To See His Goodness

MARIANNE GERDES SMITH

To See His Goodness

Copyright © 1999 by Marianne Gerdes Smith

All rights reserved. No portion of this book may be reproduced or transmitted in any form, except for brief quotations in printed reviews, without the prior permission of the publisher.

Cover by Joe Hyde and David Damico
Cover photo by Harriette Rowlandson-Baker
Book design by Marianne Smith and Joe Hyde

ISBN: 0-7392-0239-1
Library of Congress Catalog Card Number: 99-93250

Printed in the USA by

MP
MORRIS PUBLISHING

3212 East Highway 30 • Kearney, NE 68847 • 1-800-650-7888

For my son
and all those who will follow,
that generations yet to be born
may praise the Lord

I had fainted

unless I had believed to see

the goodness of the LORD

in the land of the living.

Psalm 27:13

Contents

INTRODUCTION	vviii
Crisis: Everything Is Changed Forever	1
As the Twig Is Bent	19
Those Whom God Has Joined Together	35
Boundless Realms Of Joy	46
Peering Over the Edge of Eternity	57
A Brave Bird Singing	75
The Fool Hath Said	93
Back From the Far Country	105
Equally Yoked	112
Precious In the Sight Of the Lord	123
Many Members, One Body	140
What Do You Want Me To Do For You?	149
A Lamp Unto My Feet	159
Peter, Go Ring the Bells	171
A Glimpse Of the Upper Side	182
EPILOGUE	193

Introduction

The Christian life is lived by faith, not by sight. Jesus said "Blessed are those who have not seen and yet have believed." We are given the basis of our hope in Christ in the Holy Scriptures, and are called to enter into a walk with Him by believing what He tells us there, without benefit of bells ringing, heavenly visions, or goose bumps. One who charts his spiritual pilgrimage by emotional or sensational experiences remains on shaky ground. It is not uncommon, however, for one who walks by faith in accordance with the Word of God to have experiences that confirm the truth of the Word and illuminate the spiritual dimension of his life. I have found that a good time to hear directly from the Lord is when I am tired and have ceased to consciously direct my own thought processes. In such a state of quietness and absence of striving, I can sometimes hear the "still, small voice" of the Spirit of God with an unmistakable sense of certainty.

This happened to me on the last Friday in January of 1986. I arrived home that afternoon at the end of an especially strenuous week of teaching school. On the preceding Tuesday, the nation had been shocked and saddened by the sudden and tragic deaths of seven astronauts when their space capsule exploded and disintegrated in the clear, crisp Florida sky. We had seen the accident as it happened and watched it replayed dozens of times, trying to assimilate the reality of what had taken place. It had been a hard week, and I was more ready than usual for the weekend.

The house was empty, as my son, Glenn, was away at college, and my husband, Horace, would not be home from work for another hour. I fixed my customary cup of tea, turned on the television in the den, and sat on the sofa to relax before starting supper. A newscast was reporting the memorial service for the astronauts held earlier that day at the Johnson Space Center. When President Reagan was shown comforting the families, I saw the pain and sense of helplessness in each face and was suddenly transported back twenty-two years to the time when I had stood in a similar place. My husband's reconnaissance plane, one of those famous U-2's, had fallen out of that same sky near the tip of Florida and he was lost somewhere in the water below. As I looked into each grieving face, I relived those feelings of sudden loss: inability to comprehend the fact that one with whom my life had been intricately intertwined would never come home again; knowing that no matter how much honor was bestowed on the one who was gone, *my* life was shattered; and fear of an uncertain future and feeling of inadequacy to face it alone. I was there again, standing on the brink of that ghastly chasm of grief, with those who were being shown on the screen of my television set, and my heart was filled with compassion.

Then I became conscious of an overriding and overflowing *joy*, as I realized the complete sufficiency and faithfulness of God, even in the most tragic and seemingly hopeless of circumstances. The joy came from an extreme sense of security in being in the hand of God. I could literally feel the everlasting arms. When my world fell apart at the end of 1963, I had claimed His promises and entrusted the course of my life to Him. Specifically, I asked Him to order my life so that I would be happy and fulfilled again. It seemed then that there was no way such a thing could possibly happen, but on that Friday afternoon in 1986, I saw how completely my prayer had been answered. By God's grace, I had been led into a deeply satisfying marriage; the son He gave me was a joy to my heart; I had a challenging and fulfilling job; and I was privileged to be part of a caring and committed Christian fellowship through which I served by exercising my unique gifts. My life was all together on all fronts—family, job, and church. This could have been brought about only by an all-knowing and all-loving God. It was all the more remarkable in light of the fact that there had been a period during those twenty-two years when I foolishly ceased to trust Him, became arrogant and rebellious, and ran after false gods. Amazingly, He never let me go, but gently drew me back to Himself and had truly "set my feet in a wide place." I was overcome with joy, a sense of security, and gratitude.

That experience in the solitude and quietness of my den left an afterglow that continued as my life of activity and relating to others resumed. Through the weekend, I felt as excited as a child on the night before Christmas. I marveled at each good thing in my life and thanked God for it. In church on Sunday, while I was again recounting my blessings with awe, a thought cut abruptly through my mind-wanderings like a command: *Write it all down.* When I got home from church, I wrote in my journal: "Today the idea came to me to write up an account of my experience with grief and recovery and God's wonderful hand in it all. Could this be from Him?"

At the time, I was involved in a curriculum-writing project for my school district, and any other writing was impossible, so I asked the Lord to keep the idea alive in my mind until summer if it were from Him. Otherwise, I wanted Him to cause me to forget about it. Through the spring, I thought of little else when my mind was permitted to wander freely. The opening section formed itself as I composed and recomposed portions of it. By the time the day arrived in June when I was free to sit down in my study with pencil in hand and a yellow pad before me, I could hardly keep from writing.

This story is the product of several such summers, over the course of which I graduated from yellow pad to word processor. It is told in the hope that it will show the unmistakable, loving and sure hand of God in the life of one ordinary person who dared to trust Him, however feebly at times. In the centuries-old tradition of witnessing to the truth of the gospel, "that which I have seen and heard declare I unto you." May it be a help to all who peruse these pages in more clearly seeing His goodness.

Special thanks is due to my friend, Margaret Graves, who read the first draft of the opening chapters and convinced me this was a story worth telling; to my Koinonia Group at St. Paul's Episcopal Church, who prayed and encouraged; and last, but far from least, to my husband, Horace, who gave me permission to absent myself from the present and travel back into long-forgotten corners of my heart and memory. The safe place he provides for me with his love and acceptance made it possible to do that with a clear head. In the process of the shaping of this book, he has grown accustomed to a chronically unkempt house and unhealthful, thrown-together meals. Besides all this, he generously and patiently taught me how to use his computer and then suffered interruptions at work at least daily when I called with what must have seemed to him the most elementary of questions about processing words. He doesn't know it, but I have tried to heed pearls of wisdom gleaned from his expertise as a writer—things about making words say what I mean, no more and no less. I couldn't have completed this project without him, for more reasons than I can name or even know.

Katy, Texas
August 9, 1989

With the resurrection of this manuscript in 1996, I incurred further debts toward its completion. Eleanor Reese, whom I met in the above-mentioned Koinonia group, helped immensely by proofreading and offering her thoughts and support and by occasionally prodding me to carry this book through to publication. Billie and Walter Berryhill went over the manuscript and offered many helpful suggestions. Walter discussed his thoughts with me in his hospital room as he waited to be wheeled away for hip surgery—a true labor of love. Finally, I am grateful to dozens of other friends, most notably Martha Blomquist and Eloise Smith, who read the manuscript and offered encouragement and help in making it better.

Introduction

As I was in the midst of preparing this final draft, my mother went to be with the Lord. I have to add a note of thanks to her. In addition to my life, she gave me a heritage of good sense, appreciation of people, and respect for the Almighty. I hope she will be honored by what I have written here.

Katy, Texas
October 1, 1996

1

Crisis: Everything Is Changed Forever

November 20, 1963. It was a dismal, chilly day in the Delta, that flat, fertile sweep of land in the northwestern quadrant of Mississippi nourished by the river named "Ole Man" in a wonderful song. By the time I arose on this November day, which was destined to become a stark landmark in the chronicle of my life, the sun should have shown from halfway up its path in the sky. Instead, an unbroken canopy of clouds hung just above the treetops. Everyone in the house had left to attend to various responsibilities. After I had busied myself for as long as possible with personal duties, I decided to attack a sink full of dishes left from the night before, the cook apparently having failed to come that day. As I stood at the sink with my hands in dishwater, gazing out at the leafless branches of a giant pecan tree silhouetted against the gray sky, a feeling of depression, like a wave of sadness, swept over me. It was a momentary thing, lasting just a few minutes, brought on, I thought, by dreariness and drudgery, and perhaps a touch of homesickness.

I was visiting my parents in the little Delta town of Leland, the place I still called home even though it wasn't. I had not lived there since graduating from high school a dozen years before. For half of those years I had been living the nomadic life of a military dependent. My husband, Joe Glenn Hyde, Jr., was a captain in the United States Air Force. His family and I called him Glenn, but he was known as Joe in the military. In our short time together we had lived in seven different houses, our present residence being in Tucson, where Glenn was stationed at Davis-Monthan Air Force Base. We had barely settled into our house after arriving there two months ago when he was sent to Barksdale Air Force Base in Louisiana for a temporary assignment. Actually, he requested the assignment for this particular time so he would be assured of being home in March when our first child was due to arrive. His job was to fly high altitude reconnaissance missions over Cuba in the airplane known as the U-2. He had flown the U-2 for three years and was completely satisfied and fulfilled in his work. Most of his experience with the plane had involved weather reconnaissance, which he enjoyed, but when he was assigned to take pictures of Fidel Castro's military hardware, he was elated. I had learned to be happy for him, although these missions were a cause of some anxiety for me. A year earlier, a plane from his squadron had been lost over Cuba when one of the first pilots to photograph there was shot down. I had finally been able to accept the risks of his work and usually managed not to worry about him. During this present separation, I had experienced no uneasiness about his flying, but I was counting the days until he would be finished and we could go back to Arizona and get on with our life together. Barksdale was close enough to Leland that he could drive over often on weekends, but being together at home would be much better.

As the gloomy day wore on, I retained a mood to match it. It was a relief when darkness closed in, because I could look forward to some diversion with the arrival of guests. My mother was entertaining her book club that night. After supper, she lay down to rest for a few minutes and I sat down in the living room by the fire to read the paper. The quietness of the evening was interrupted by the two tones of the door bell, and I went to answer it, expecting to greet an early arriving book club member. When I opened the door, I was surprised to see two friends from my husband's squadron, Tony Martinez and George Bull. I greeted them like old friends, which of course they were. It was wonderful to have contact with the world that I loved, and I was really glad to see them.

So many thoughts can flash through one's mind in a split second. Glenn had mentioned in one of his letters that he might bring some of the men from his unit at Barksdale over one weekend to go deer hunting. Although this was Wednesday, not the weekend, I thought, when I saw Tony and George, that they had come for a hunting trip, and I expected Glenn to jump out from behind a bush. That would have been like him. He could hardly make an entrance or initiate a telephone conversation without some kind of joke. I should have suspected something serious when I saw the men in uniform, but uniforms seem normal when you live with them every day. I invited them in and in a few seconds heard Tony say, "Marianne, I'm afraid we have some bad news." Then it hit me—this was no social call. He proceeded to tell me that Glenn had taken off early that morning and had flown a routine mission over the target area. On his return trip, at about 11:00 a.m., his plane had disappeared from the radar screen that was tracking him. Later an oil slick was discovered in the area, about forty miles from Key West in the Gulf of Mexico. There was a possibility he had ejected and could be alive. A search was underway.

As the reality of what I was hearing began to sink in, my knees became weak and I remember a feeling of helplessness coming over me. I was facing what for me at that time was the ultimate crisis. Naturally I chose to assume that he was alive, but from the beginning, I knew his chances for survival were not good. Glenn's flying and the possibility of a mishap was a problem I had struggled with since we started going together in 1957. At a point early in our marriage I had made a decision not to allow the time we had together to be clouded by my dwelling on the danger and staying in a state of anxiety. I accepted the possibility that I could lose him, but I received the assurance that if that happened, the Lord was able to see me through even that. He proved Himself faithful in the first moments of crisis. Just as I felt myself sinking under the shock, I received an infusion of energy and felt myself being literally carried along.

First I had to go and tell Mama what had happened. She joined us in the living room as we planned the practical steps to be taken. She had to make a call to cancel the meeting that was due to convene at her house in a matter of minutes. (The grapevine operates so well in Leland that only one lady failed to get the message in time.) Then I needed to get in touch with Ruth and Joe Hyde, Glenn's parents in LaGrange, Georgia. Tony wanted this done as quickly as possible as they were delaying notification of the news media about the crash until the family had been contacted. I knew exactly how to do this. On our last visit to LaGrange, we had attended church with Mr. and Mrs. Hyde, as we did every time we were there on a Sunday. They were pillars of the First Baptist Church and adored their pastor, Thornton Williams. Sitting in that service, the thought had come to me that if anything should ever happen to Glenn I should call Mr. Williams first. As I walked into the next room to use the telephone, feeling as if I were floating across the floor, I remember thinking to myself, "I can't believe I'm this calm; when am I going to crack up?" It was truly not in my own strength.

I was unable to reach Mr. Williams the first time I tried. Tony didn't think we could wait much longer, so, much against my better judgment, I placed a call to the Hyde residence, hoping no one would answer. I knew they would need some support when they received the news. Thankfully, there was no answer, but later we were able to reach the associate pastor, Mr. Graves, who found the pastor and relayed the news to him. Mr. Williams went to the small neighborhood grocery store Mr. Hyde was running at the time and found them both there in the process of closing up. She told me later that he held both of their hands and told them about the accident. She said they received so much strength from his being there. That stands out for me as a beautiful example of the Lord never forsaking His own. They called me when they got home to let me know they had been notified. We encouraged each other and agreed to look for good news.

Tony called Barksdale to instruct them to release the story, and it was reported on the ten o'clock news. The first person we heard from was my sister, Rachel, who was a student at Millsaps College. She called to tell me she loved me. Then my cousin, Bill Weilenman, appeared at the door. He had heard the news on the radio as he was getting ready for bed. He has always been a strong support for our family in good times and bad, and he and I are especially close. It was good to have him there.

Earlier in the evening, my mother had called a local physician and friend, Dr. Carl Nichols. Her first concern, of course, was for my physical well-being and that of the baby. Carl and I had become acquainted four years before when he attended me during a miscarriage. He joined our little group in the living room.

I don't know how long we sat there carrying on small talk and acting as though the telephone might ring at any moment with news of the search in the Gulf of Mexico. Finally, Carl gave me some pills that he said would help me to sleep, told me to call him if I needed anything, and excused himself. We prepared beds upstairs for George and Tony, Bill said good night and went home, and we all turned in for the evening. I don't remember having any trouble sleeping. Maybe I took one of those little pills.

The next day, Tony went back to Barksdale and George remained to await further developments. I expected to hear something that very day, and I didn't let the notion slip into my consciousness that it would be anything but good news. We did hear that the plane was found and that the cockpit was empty, indicating that the pilot might have ejected. I told an Associated Press reporter in a telephone interview that afternoon that I was a stubborn optimist, that I thought my husband was all right, and that I refused to believe anything different yet.

My family began to come together. My sister, Corinne, and Baby Nathan arrived from Memphis, followed by my brother, Leo, from Montgomery. Then Rachel came from Jackson. The little town of Leland rallied to the crisis, as it always does in such cases, and friends came by the dozens, bringing us encouragement and good food. My mother has a rare gift of hospitality and people always have a good time at her house. Even in the midst of these trying circumstances, she was able to create an atmosphere in which people enjoyed each other and were refreshed from having been together. I was uplifted many times by these heartfelt visits. At other times I probably seemed downright rude when I retreated to my room in despair. Those were times when the reality of the situation I was facing would roll over me like a flood.

On Friday, November 22, I was the first to arise and brought in the morning paper, the Memphis *Commercial Appeal*. The headlines carried the story we had heard the day before: *U-2 Wreckage Found; Empty Cockpit Keeps Hope Alive For Pilot*. There was an official Air Force photograph of Glenn that was to become all too familiar in the days ahead. Inside was a picture of me that had run six years earlier in the Society Section to announce my engagement and a story about my "stubborn optimism". The front page also carried a picture of President and Mrs. Kennedy and Texas Governor and Mrs. Connally riding in a motorcade in San Antonio.

At lunchtime, we were seated at the table when the phone rang and my father got up to answer it. Our neighbor, Frances Crowe, was calling. We heard Daddy say something about a joke. He obviously thought she was kidding. But then he became serious and began asking questions like "What time?" and "Do they know who did it?" When he hung up, he turned and said, "Somebody just shot the president." That was our introduction to the tragedy in Dallas.

From that time forward, we stayed glued to the television set as we watched the drama in Dallas and

Washington unfold in black and white before our eyes. The accused assassin died in a shoot-out in a Dallas jail. A new president was sworn in aboard a jetliner bound for Washington. A fallen president was borne through the streets of the nation's capitol by horse-drawn hearse and laid to rest in the National Cemetery. A young widow conducted herself with dignity, grace, and a sense of history. And a nation mourned.

Through it all, I continued to await news of the search for my missing husband off the tip of Florida. As the days wore on, I began gradually to accept the fact that the person I loved most in the world was indeed lost to me. During those very difficult days, my friends were the source of much strength and encouragement. In addition to the concern expressed by people in Leland, I received telephone calls from across the country, as people read the story behind the headlines. The postman delivered stacks of mail that encouraged and comforted. During one of my moves in later years, in a fit of simplifying and streamlining my household possessions, I threw away most of those letters. I wish I had them now, but I did find recently a sheaf of telegrams received at the time that contain the essence of the communications that came my way by letter and telephone. One especially touching one came from Ann and Chuck Stratton. Chuck had achieved fame by parachuting from a distressed U-2 one night, landing in a tree in southern Mississippi, and staying there until morning. Ann was a good friend of mine, and I had taught their two boys in first grade at East Side School in Del Rio, Texas, when we were all stationed at Laughlin Air Force Base. This is what they wired:

Chucky and Bobby had Joe in mind when they said their prayers last night. Also the rest of us. Keep your chin up. God bless you. Ann and Chuck Stratton.

I did try to keep my chin up, and I was helped tremendously in this by friends like these who stood with me. On the scene with me was a very good friend, Bettyann, who had married my cousin, Bill, after losing her first husband in the Korean War. It gave me hope to witness her rebuilt life. She obviously had been able to enter into a second good marriage and had a happy family. They had a daughter from her first marriage as well as four other children. I wonder now how she was able to spend so much time with me with so much going on at home. We spent hours together then and continue to be good friends to this day.

We were kept very well informed on the progress of the search by telephone. In addition, official progress reports came by telegram from the wing commander, Col. John DesPortes. On November 22, I received the following message:

> The search for your husband Joe is continuing both by aircraft and surface vessels. My director of operations Colonel T. J. Jackson is at Key West closely monitoring the search and is keeping me constantly advised. You will be informed immediately of any important development in the progress of the search. Please feel free to contact me any time I can be of assistance.

On November 25, the following update came by telegram:

> This is to inform you officially that your husband is still missing and the search for him is continuing. I will keep you informed of any new developments.

Again, please contact me at any time if I can be of assistance.

Finally, on November 29, I was notified that the search had been suspended in a telegram that came as no surprise or shock:

> This is to inform you that the massive intensive sea and surface search for your husband has been suspended after a complete coverage of the area and for the lack of any leads that would warrant further search of this magnitude at this time. Your husband is still considered as missing and all air and surface search is on standby to immediately renew their search efforts if any new leads develop. I regret that our efforts to date have not developed any leads.

The following day, November 30, 1963, the Air Force decided to declare Captain Joe Glenn Hyde, Jr. dead. A telegram from his parents to me reflects the sorrow felt by all of us who loved him:

> May God's grace and infinite love surround us all in this dark hour. Isaiah 26:3. We love you dearly. Mama Ruth and Daddy Joe.

The scripture reference, which I immediately looked up and marked in my Bible, says *Thou wilt keep him in perfect peace whose mind is stayed on thee, because he trusteth in thee.* It was to set the tone for the way I would face the adjustment that awaited me and has remained one of my most treasured passages from the Word of God.

I had grown to accept this thing that had happened, at least in my head, partly because I had previously "tried on the idea" of losing my husband when I walked through similar losses with friends. Although I believed it would never really happen, I *had* at least looked the possibility in the face. The fact remained, however, that my heart was broken, my world had fallen apart, and I didn't know what I was going to do or how I could possibly establish a new life that would be anywhere near acceptable. Fortunately, the immediate decisions were made for me. We had to go to LaGrange for a memorial service in Glenn's home town, and then I would return to Leland and stay with my parents at least until my baby was born.

The date for the memorial service was set for Saturday, December 7. There would be simultaneous services at the First Baptist Church in LaGrange and in the chapel at Davis-Monthan Air Force Base in Arizona. I flew to Georgia the day before, escorted by dear George, who by this time had been away from his family and work for more than two weeks. He never showed the slightest displeasure with the unusual and unexpected duty he had been assigned, but I know it was not easy being in limbo for so many days. Our neighbors, Bonnie and Sid McKnight, opened their home and hearts to him during his stay in Leland, which gave him some much needed relief from the activity and tension at our house. I must say that having him on the scene during that time was an invaluable support for me, for which I was most grateful. Needless to say, the two of us became very well acquainted. He had been one of Glenn's good friends, and I considered his wife, Martha, one of my closest friends at the time. Their daughter, Susan, had studied piano with me when we lived in Del Rio. So George and I were far from strangers at the outset of the ordeal we endured together, but our friendship deepened as a result of it.

Walking into the home of Ruth and Joe Hyde was the first of many painful returns to places Glenn and I had experienced together. We had spent many happy hours at the comfortable old house on Harwell Avenue.

There had been leisurely hours sitting on the front porch in the swing or in wicker chairs talking in the cool of the evening. The back porch brought back scenes of summertime meals consisting of an assortment of fresh vegetables from Joe Hyde's garden and ending with the famous Hyde pound cake. In spite of the intense feeling of loss brought on by this flood of memories, I was glad to be there. Since the first time I met Glenn's family I had felt nothing but warmth and acceptance, and being with them was overwhelmingly comforting. We cried together, laughed together, and received half the city of LaGrange in the living room during the short time I was there.

The house was full of family—Glenn's sister, Betty Anne, and brother, Richard, their spouses and children, all totaling eleven people. Mrs. Hyde's mother, Frances Gordy, whom we called MaMa, lived there and added a sparkle to the whole scene with her humor and wisdom.

I don't know where everyone slept, but MaMa slept with her daughter so I could have her room. That night, while I enjoyed the luxury of a private room, I finally gave in to the grief I had been carrying so stoically. Before I got into bed, I opened a copy of the LaGrange paper. There was that familiar official photograph of my beloved husband, accompanied by a write-up of his death and plans for the service the following day. And there I stood, five months pregnant with his child and wondering how this terrible thing could possibly have happened. I cried way into the night. There would be other times when the reality of the loss would hit me as if for the first time, but that night, when I first allowed myself to feel and respond to my grief, was the beginning of a long process of healing.

As strange as it may seem, I enjoyed the memorial service. A planeload of men from the 4080th Strategic Wing came. They were beautiful in their uniforms as they lined the curved stairway up to the church while people entered. The church was filled for what to me was a celebration of life, not a ritual of death. When the family walked up to the front after everyone else was seated, I was thinking of Jackie Kennedy. I wanted to represent my husband with the kind of dignity and honor I had seen in her. I wore a black wool maternity dress that I happened to be making at the time of the accident. It is strange that I should have chosen black material to sew, because it is not a good color for me and I never wear it. While I don't think it is necessary to wear black as a symbol of mourning, in this particular instance it seemed appropriate and I was glad I had the dress. As we walked down the aisle, I stood tall, held my head up, and attempted to act out for myself, as well as for anyone who was looking, my conviction that Glenn's life was something to be thankful for and that there was fullness of joy in store for those of us who loved him.

Reverend Thornton Williams put his whole heart into writing and conducting the service. He read portions of Psalms 27 and 138 that reiterated God's ever-presence with his children, especially in times of trouble. His opening message ended with a statement of the truth on which I was resting all my hope. How good it was to hear it proclaimed by God's messenger: *As God has been with us in all our yesterdays, He will be with us in our today, and in the unknown tomorrows.* Those unknown tomorrows were already beginning to give me no small amount of concern.

The eulogy included accounts by various people in the community who had known Glenn well. His high school coach, a professional man who had officiated at football games in which he played, the superintendent of schools, a Sunday school teacher, a pastor, and a former employer all testified to Glenn's character, integrity, loyalty, good humor, and the fine example he set for young people.

It was reported that on Sunday, November 11, 1941, at the age of eleven, he made a profession of faith in Jesus Christ and was baptized that same Sunday. I was grateful to the Baptists for being so meticulous in recording such things. It gave assurance that he was in the presence of the Father at that very moment. That had been one of the first questions I grappled with after his death. I knew the Christian teaching on eternal life and was reasonably sure Glenn possessed it, but this was the first time I had had to trust that what the Bible says was true for a significant person in my life.

My doubts about Glenn's eternal destiny were finally settled as a result of a very interesting dream I had shortly after receiving confirmation of his death. In my dream, I had driven him to the flight line at Laughlin Air Force Base, as I had done so many times when he was to leave on cross-countries in the T-33. It was a very familiar scene, only this time, although he was wearing a flight suit, he was not going to take off in a plane, but would be walking up a steep hill on a gravel road. As he got out of the car to leave, I said to him, "Now, when you get to the top of that hill, Jesus is going to be waiting for you with open arms." His answer came back like a flash: "You don't have to tell me that; I've already been there." I woke up laughing at myself for assuming the role of his spiritual guardian (which I was always inclined to do), and knowing deep within myself that what I had heard in that dream was absolutely true. I never had another uneasy moment in regard to what had become of him when his spirit left his body that day in November over the Gulf of Mexico.

I hasten to say that I don't believe Glenn actually spoke to me in that dream. I think my statement to him came from deep in my subconscious, because I *know* that had I had the opportunity to say one more thing to him, I would have expressed that very thought. I think his answer to me came from the Holy Spirit. It had a ring of truth to it that I cannot deny even today, a quarter of a century later. It remains one of the most precious spiritual experiences of my life.

The eulogy continued with a tribute from his commanding officer, which is quoted in its entirety as follows:

Twenty-two years ago today brave men at Pearl Harbor gave their lives for this country. Today we pay respect to another brave man who also gave his life for his country.

    JOE GLENN HYDE, JR.
    Captain, United States Air Force

    As an officer—
        Dedicated, dependable, one of the finest

    As a combat Crew of the Strategic Air Command—
        Competent, reliable, eager

    As an individual—
        A gentleman, great physical and moral stature

    As a citizen—
        A great representative of his state, his alma mater, and his country

    As a man—
        Honest, confident, proud of his heritage, a pillar of strength

    As a friend—
        Loyal, inspirational, sincere

    As an American—
        Who could rank higher than Joe Glenn Hyde, Jr. who gave his life for us all in the cause of freedom?

Mr. Williams closed with a meditation on John 15:13: *Greater love hath no man than this, that a man lay down his life for his friends.* He spoke of our forefathers' dream of a land of freedom and how they faithfully worked to make such a dream come true. Then he linked Glenn with that dream in these sentences:

> We have kept such freedom only at an unbelievable cost of human bravery. Is the dream worth keeping? Is it worth self-sacrifice? We honor one today who answered yes, not only with his lips but with his life.

I pondered that idea for a long time. It seemed to me that Glenn enjoyed what he did too much to receive so much honor for it. I wasn't sure that he performed those hazardous missions out of a dedication to freedom so much as for the joy and satisfaction he got from it. Life was so ordinary for us. I don't think he felt like a hero. He simply went to work and did a job he loved doing. There was never a lot of talk about serving the country. I see it differently now. The fact that he gained personal satisfaction from his work does not change the fact that bringing back those photographs of an adversary's military landscape helped the cause of freedom, and for that he should be honored. Furthermore, I don't believe he would have submitted to the acknowledged risks had he not believed strongly in the importance to his country of what he was doing. He was a hero in every sense of the word, and his children's children can take pride in that heritage for as long as the story is told.

The service ended on a triumphant note, and the men from Davis-Monthan joined us at the Hyde house. It was like being surrounded by a group of big brothers. They treated me with so much kindness and respect, and I was proud to be able to introduce them to the family as my friends. The day was an uplifting one for me.

Later that evening, after all the visitors had left, Mama Ruth and I were in the living room alone and *we hit bottom together.* I didn't realize then how devastating her grief must have been. The structure of my life had fallen apart, but she had lost a son. What could be more heartbreaking? Within seven years, she would die of cancer, and I can't help thinking that the disease was somehow brought on by her deep sorrow. That night, though, the thoughts she expressed were for me, not herself. She said, "Marianne, I just feel so sorry for you." At that point I joined her in weeping and said, "I know I'll be happy again, Mama Ruth, but I don't see how." It was by the grace of God that I had the assurance, in the midst of so great a loss, that life was still good. He had been preparing me for this for a long time.

2

As the Twig is Bent

Leland is a little town in the Mississippi Delta that sprang up a century ago beside the Yazoo and Mississippi Valley Railroad as a trading center for the emerging cotton industry. Through the middle of town runs Deer Creek, the object of beautification efforts for years. It has repaid the attention given to it many times over, giving Leland its reputation as a beauty spot. The lighted trees and colorful floats expressing the spirit of Christmas every winter have made Leland's Deer Creek famous for miles around. There used to be a sign outside of town that said "5000 nice people and a few old soreheads welcome you to Leland." Time has erased the memory of any soreheads, but I can attest to the nice people. This is the place where I was privileged to spend the first eighteen years of my life, and it was in this place that I had woven into the fabric of my consciousness a spiritual perspective that has markedly affected the course of my life. It was the value system instilled in me during those early years that enabled me to meet my first major disappointment, the death of my husband, with a measure of faith and a determination to keep going.

It all began when I first saw the light of day in the Greenville Kings Daughters Hospital a few days after Franklin Roosevelt became the thirty-second President of the United States. My mother, the former Cora Weilenman, was in the third generation of a pioneer Delta family. My father, Leo Gerdes, was a Texan by birth, whose German grandparents immigrated there in the middle of the last century. After graduating from Texas A&M College (now University) in 1928, he went to work with the United States Department of Agriculture in Washington as a cotton technologist. He was later assigned to direct the technological division of the U. S. Cotton Ginning Laboratory being set up in Stoneville, Mississippi, near Leland, where he met and married my mother in 1932.

Growing up in Leland was a privilege I did not fully appreciate until recently, as I have witnessed the progressive secularization of our society. Leland in the 1930's and '40's was a community with a Christian consensus, although it did not start out that way. In the years after its founding in 1886, it was notorious for its numerous saloons and accompanying lawlessness. An article in a national magazine in 1908 described it as the "hellhole of the Delta."[1] In spite of the negative elements associated with its beginnings, however, the town's early settlers came with strong moral and spiritual ideals, and the history of Leland is marked by a series of church foundings. The scene that I came upon was one where the churches were central in the life of the community.

---

1 Dorothy Love Turk, Leland, Mississippi: From Hellhole to Beauty Spot. (Leland, Mississippi: Leland Historical Foundation, 1986) p. 34.

I grew up in the Methodist Church. A pair of stained-glass windows that I studied during countless church services are inscribed to the memory of my grandmother, Maydell Latham Weilenman, and my great-grandmother, Margaret Amanda Weilenman. Margaret Amanda became a widow when my grandfather, Willie Elijah, the second youngest of her eight children, was a small boy. She brought her family to the Delta in 1874 when it was in its primeval state of swampland and forest. Her youngest child, Mattie, who, at the age of five, accompanied her mother and her five sisters to the Delta from their former home below Vicksburg, wrote an account of the move before her death in 1954. She described the glittering steamboat in which they traveled and told of the anxious days of waiting for the men of the family, two brothers, as they made the trip overland with wagons loaded with their household goods and livestock, including seventy-five head of cattle, trailing behind. The wait ended on a lovely springtime morning when they heard a cowbell in the distance. One of the first things Margaret Amanda did after the family was reunited was to call everyone in for scripture reading and prayers. Those prayers must have rung with thanksgiving for the safe passage of her children through country that harbored many a hazard. She later became one of the founders of the Leland Methodist Church in 1897. The cornerstone of the present building of the church shows my grandfather's name as chairman of the Board of Stewards at the time it was laid in 1923.

Although my Methodist roots are deep, I am indebted to the Lord's whole church for nurturing my spiritual life, because many denominations have contributed to the growth of my faith. My father was a Roman Catholic. I never attended that church, but that was where I was baptized as an infant. My grandmother, Antonia Meyer Gerdes, saw to that. When my parents carried me to Daddy's hometown of Sinton, Texas, for the first time, Grandma arranged for me to be baptized at the church where she was a parishioner. I'm grateful for that. I'm glad my grandmother thought it was important to place me formally in the family of God. I think that is an appropriate concern for grandparents. It's not that parents are not concerned; but like Martha, the sister of Mary in the Bible, they are often "careful and troubled about many things," while the older generation, if they are wise, have learned to choose "that good part" which endures. Entering, as I am, the age of the older generation, I find that I pick up on things of eternal import that previously went unnoticed. For instance, in a recent Service of Holy Baptism in my church, which happened to be conducted by the bishop, I heard, as if for the first time, the words "...you are sealed by the Holy Spirit in Baptism and marked as Christ's own forever." What powerful words to speak over a helpless little baby! Of course the child must make his own decision later in life as to how he will respond to the gift of salvation, but the sacrament surely predisposes his heart to seek the Lord. The priest in Sinton no doubt said similar words over me, albeit in Latin. Although I have taken many wrong turns and gone through periods of rebellion and foolishness in regard to God, basically my heart has always been turned toward Him.

During my years of growing up, I attended numerous revivals and vacation Bible schools at the Baptist and Presbyterian churches in Leland, as well as those in my own church. At various times, when the invitation was given, I had a strong urge to go down the aisle at Baptist revivals, but never did because I was a Methodist. I had some good Sunday school teachers in my own church, and every time I sang the little chorus "Into My Heart" from the old *Cokesbury Hymnal,* I really asked Jesus to "come in today, come in to stay."

With the life of the town revolving around its churches, it is no surprise that the school promoted spiritual values. Along with the Pledge of Allegiance every morning, there were classroom devotionals with Bible reading, prayer, and hymn-singing, and the school superintendent's wife, Mrs. Bufkin, came regularly and read Bible stories to the elementary school children all gathered in the auditorium. That anyone would object to these practices was inconceivable. We understood the values they represented to be foundational to our way of life.

Somewhere in the course of my childhood, I crossed over into the kingdom of light, but I've never been able to pinpoint an exact moment. By the time I was a teenager, I knew that God had a plan for my life and truly wanted to find it, but I didn't really understand salvation. (Of course, no one ever really understands salvation on this side of the veil, but we do grow in grace as we seek to live into it.)

When I was sixteen, my mother did a wonderful thing for me and sent me to camp for the summer. I didn't think it so was wonderful when she first suggested it, however. My friends and I were enjoying that sense of liberation that comes with newly acquired drivers' licenses, and I was looking forward to a summer of talking on the telephone and driving up and down the road socializing (but not at the same time—this was pre-cellular). My mother had other ideas, which were, of course, better and enrolled my sister Corinne and me at Camp Montreat, a girls' summer camp located on the beautiful Presbyterian assembly grounds at Montreat, North Carolina, in the Blue Ridge Mountains. In spite of my lack of enthusiasm, it turned out to be an enriching experience that left many lasting impressions. The camp director was a widow named Mrs. S. H. McBride, whom we called Macky. She told me years later when I visited her on a trip through western North Carolina that she chose to run a girls' camp, rather than one for boys, because she believed she could have more influence on homes by providing direction for future mothers. Macky did everything with style and ceremony and worked to make camp a place where we learned new things, established deep friendships, and had fun, but her larger goal was that we learn to live our lives based on a strong spiritual foundation.

One of my most vivid memories is of her method of waking us up in the morning. She would sit in one of the straight-backed rocking chairs on the long porch across the front of the dining hall and sing a little chorus to the tune of "Count Your Blessings": *Read your Bible, read it everyday; Read your Bible, read it come what may; Read your Bible, read it every day; Read your precious Bible, read it everyday.* This gave those of us who were not too sound asleep to hear her a chance to have a quiet time before the wake-up bell sounded about fifteen minutes later. My bunk was next to a window in the building adjacent to the dining hall, so I always heard her. Many mornings I sat up and read my Bible, but my guess is that there were as many days when I went back to sleep. Even so, this was when I learned that having a quiet time early in the morning is a good thing, and I have tried since then, with varying degrees of success, to set that time aside for God.

Macky's many-faceted program of camp activities included regular times of Bible study. She was so old-fashioned that she believed in memorizing scripture. I still have the Bible I used at camp, and on the fly-leaf is written her Bible alphabet with a verse beginning with each letter of the alphabet. Many of those verses, especially those near the beginning of the list, are still available in my memory for immediate recall and have come to me at various times through the years when I have needed them: *A: A soft answer turneth away wrath, but grievous words stir up anger,* Proverbs 15:1, *B: Be ye kind one to another, tenderhearted, forgiving one another, even as God for Christ's sake hath forgiven you,* Ephesians 4:32, *C: Create in me a clean heart, O God, and renew a right spirit within me,* Psalm 51:10, *etc.* The verses taken as a whole are a rich arsenal of truth for a young person to have at his fingertips. Reviewing them makes me wish I had not been, like Martha, so "careful and troubled about many things" when my own child was at the age to learn such things. Maybe I'll be given another chance when the next generation comes along.

Another way Macky sought to feed our souls was through "Hayloft Talks" every Sunday night. After a supper of peanut butter sandwiches, which we called "slow death", we would gather in the upper story of one of the residences, the Hayloft, clad in pajamas and supplied with hair brushes and bobby pins. There, while we brushed and rolled up our hair, Macky told us about herself. I guess you could say she "gave her testimony", but that description hardly conveys the intensity and drama of her story as she told it to us. She had no problem keeping the attention of her young audience when she told of falling in love with Sam, the wonderful young man she had married many years before. She told us how it felt to know she had met God's chosen mate for her and how blissful was their courtship and later their marriage. These things, told by one who had lived out what for most of us amounted to a "heart's desire" struck a deep note of responsiveness. This made us all the more empathetic when she told of Sam's untimely death as the result of an accident, leaving her with two small children. It was a precious thing when this saintly woman, who must have been in her fifties at the time, reached into her rich store of experience and shared the shock, grief, doubts, fears, and faith she experienced in facing this tragedy with the group of insignificant children that we were. Of course she knew we were not insignificant, and she was wise enough to know that this was the kind of input that would shape values and strengthen spiritual resources in her girls as no amount of instruction could. She let us know how heartbroken she was when Sam died, but she also showed us that God was sufficient even in these devastating circumstances, for she credited Him with healing her grief and giving her a full and meaningful life. Those talks made a tremendous impression on me. It is a marvel to me that the Lord knew then, when I was only sixteen, what lay ahead for me and had begun even then to give me what I would need to face it.

During that summer at Montreat in 1949, we traveled over to the nearby Baptist assembly grounds at Ridgecrest to hear a young preacher named Billy Graham. I can't remember much about the event except Macky's excitement. He would receive national attention through his crusade in California the following fall. We campers didn't know at the time what a significant Christian figure we were privileged to hear, but I think Macky knew.

The following year, she built her own camp, Camp Merri-Mac, on the side of a mountain in Black Mountain, a short distance from the entrance to Montreat. In June, Macky's girls gathered in a newly built cluster of buildings especially planned for her kind of program. To this day, whenever I smell fresh lumber I am transported back to the summer of 1950 and Sunnyside Cabin. I attended Merri-Mac for two summers, and then I went to college.

Stephens College in 1951 was a quaint place even compared with most schools of its time, and surely with those of today. Closing time in the dorms was 10:30 and "lights out" was at 11:00 on week nights. I think it was stretched a little on weekends. Stephens girls were not allowed to ride in cars, and they were required to go to church on Sunday. We registered for the church we preferred and turned in an IBM card on Sunday morning to prove we were there. I chose the Missouri Methodist Church in Columbia, where for the first time I heard "real" organ music, and I thought it was wonderful. The organ music I had grown up with had issued forth from a Hammond organ and consisted mostly of transcriptions of popular classics. To hear the music of Bach and other great masters played on a pipe organ was a whole new world for me. The second semester found me taking organ as a minor instrument.

My major was piano, which meant my life revolved around the music building, Gauntlett Hall. My piano teacher, Richard Johnson, was head of the piano department, and I and everyone else he taught all but worshipped him. He had taught my high school piano teacher, Polly Applewhite, and took me as a pupil on her recommendation. Otherwise, he surely would have assigned me to someone else, because I was not in the same league as his other students. Being one of the best piano players in Leland High School had given me a certain amount of confidence, but here I was being compared with the best players from across the country and I fell far short. I struggled to keep up, and I must say Mr. Johnson gave me some excellent instruction, including some, no doubt, that went right over my head. My strong subjects were music theory and other courses dealing with the intellectual side of music, and

I loved the small, intimate classes. For many of them, we met in the comfortable, homey studio of the music department head, Dr. Peter Hansen, and besides receiving a very fine musical foundation there, I made some lifelong friends. One of these was a girl from my home state named Peggy Wright. She and I later roomed together at Louisiana State University, where we went for our last two years of college.

At L. S. U. my life again was centered in the music building, with countless hours spent in the practice rooms on the third floor. I joined a sorority, which served as the focus of my social life, and was active in the Wesley Foundation at University Methodist Church.

It was near the end of my senior year that I met a lady who was going to have a very strong influence on me through the years in many important ways. Her name was Catherine Marshall, and I met her in a movie called *A Man Called Peter,* which was based on the biography she wrote of her husband, Peter Marshall. Just as I had vicariously lived Macky's story, so I lived Catherine's as she fell in love with and married the young Scottish-born preacher. In the movie, Peter became Chaplain of the United States Senate while he was serving as minister at the historic New York Avenue Presbyterian Church in the nation's capitol. At the height of a most fruitful ministry, he was struck down by a heart attack. I cried in the movie as if his death were my own loss. I immediately got a copy of the book and can remember sitting propped up in my bed in West Hall with tears streaming down my face reading the last chapter, "See You in the Morning," which were Catherine's last words to her husband. Little did I know then that the author of that book would show me, more than anyone else, how to live again after a similar loss in my own life.

A Bachelor of Music degree in applied piano gave me much pleasure in the pursuing of it and satisfaction in the completion of it, but it did not open the door to many career opportunities. I should have majored in music education, but I could not bear to forsake the School of Music for that of Education. That's why I considered myself fortunate to be hired by the school in Shaw, Mississippi, as a piano teacher. The school provided one of the rooms behind the stage of the auditorium for a studio and paid me a small stipend for playing the piano for school functions. The remainder of my income came from fees paid by parents for private lessons.

I have fond memories of my year in Shaw. Four other teachers and I rented a house (one of the "teachers' houses") across the street from the school. My roommate, LaNelle Hill, a new graduate of Mississippi State College for Women, became another of my lifelong friends. She taught what we used to call public school music in grades one through twelve, so our jobs overlapped. I played for her programs, and we worked up some two-piano music, which we performed at my recitals.

LaNelle and I also learned to cook together. We were the only new teachers to move into the teachers' house that year, and we soon learned that we had become a part of a highly structured organization. We were horrified to find out that every five weeks one person was responsible for planning, shopping for, and preparing breakfast and dinner for the household. Neither of us had done much cooking beyond making cookies, but as our weeks of responsibility approached, we consulted with our mothers, gathered recipes from various sources, and were ready. Many of those recipes I still have on cards in a recipe file I started then. I was amazed recently to read a week's menu I found on a folded paper in the back of that file box. The evening meals included roast beef, ham, or chicken, with a full complement of side dishes. Breakfast was different every day, with biscuits, pancakes, or muffins to accompany poached, scrambled or fried eggs and various breakfast meats—and always grits. I surely don't plan that well today, using the excuse that I don't have time with teaching full time! (Just ask my husband.)

In spite of the good things about that first year of independence, it was in many ways a difficult year. My life had been programmed through college. I knew what I would be doing until I finished school. Beyond that, I had always thought that the next thing would be meeting Prince Charming, marrying him, and living happily ever after. With such a mindset, it is natural that I thought the young man I was dating when I graduated was that person. As it turned out, ours was a match that was not to be, and I went through considerable misery before the relationship was finally resolved to the satisfaction of all. This basically carefree and fulfilling time of my life was interrupted by periods of depression and general anxiety about the future, the happiness of which I thought hung on the course of this particular relationship. I think this was the first time I had experienced the frustration that comes from facing a seemingly insurmountable problem, and it is the first time I can remember turning to God with a specific need. All I really wanted to do was get married, establish a home, and raise a family, and that goal seemed unreachable.

Remembering my early training about seeking God in the early morning, I started going to my studio before any other teachers arrived at school. Sitting with my knees next to the ancient radiator as it began to bring forth heat amidst a din of clanging and hissing, I had a "quiet time". I was using at that time a small volume of the Berkeley New Testament, and it was from this book that I first had a sense of the Lord speaking directly to me. As I approached Him about the seeming dead end I had reached, the words of James 1:2-4 took on special meaning:

> Consider it wholly joyful, my brothers, when you get involved in all sorts of trials, well aware that the testing of your faith brings out steadfastness. But let steadfastness have full play, so that you may be completed and rounded out with no defects whatever.

That meant to me that I should be thankful to have come upon something I couldn't handle, because this gave me an opportunity to see God work it out and thereby strengthen my faith. That faith, I might add, was pitifully weak, especially when it came to believing that God would act specifically in my situation; but thanks be to God, it takes only a shred of faith for Him to work.

In the spring of that year, the Music Placement Office at L. S. U. sent me a notice of a class piano job opening in the Highland Park Independent School District in Dallas. The idea of seeking our fortunes in a city like Dallas appealed to LaNelle and me, so the day after the close of school, we set out for "Big D" in my parents' station wagon for job interviews. She was hired by the Dallas Independent School District to teach elementary music, and I got the Highland Park job.

It was wonderful being in Texas. I sensed a change in the air as soon as we crossed the border at Texarkana. The roads, the sky, and the people all seemed bigger. Having grown up with my father singing the praises of the "great state of Texas" undoubtedly conditioned me for this response, but my feelings about the Lone Star State have never changed.

We moved into an apartment on East Binkley between the S. M. U. campus and the Central Expressway with two of LaNelle's friends from college, Janet Smith and Sylvia Duck, who had come to town to work for the Dallas Public Library. I thought my world had come together in Dallas. My roommate from L. S. U., Peggy, was a flight attendant with American Airlines and lived out by Love Field. My childhood friend from Leland, Jane Standefer, also flew with American and lived in our apartment complex.

One night LaNelle and I attended a church supper downtown at First Methodist Church, and who should be there but Flora Dell Davis, a friend from Stephens who had been in all those music classes with me. She was working at the church and her fiancé, John Tedford, was assistant organist. We saw a lot of each other that year.

A friend from college, Warren Blakemon, was attending the Perkins School of Theology at S. M. U. For the Texas State Fair in October, he got a job narrating the Lincoln Continental exhibit. When he found out his employers needed some models for the exhibit, he procured the job for me and an S. M. U. coed he knew. As inexperienced and unsophisticated as I was, I hate to think of the sad job I must have done, but when I was paid nearly as much for working evenings for two weeks as I earned in a month at my teaching job, it gave me an idea for augmenting my meager income. Shortly after the close of the fair, I embarked upon my big project of the year by enrolling in a modeling school. Classes met two evenings a week, and my personal image was considerably enhanced thereby.

On another evening each week, LaNelle and I drove to the auditorium at Fair Park to usher for the Dallas Symphony Orchestra concerts. At that time, area music teachers worked the concerts in exchange for free admission. That left one week night, Thursday, which found me at choir practice at First Methodist. The weekends were always busy with social engagements of one kind or another. It was a most exciting year, like living at the center of the universe. Each time I've visited Dallas in the years since, a drive through the streets of Highland Park has given me a poignant pang of nostalgia as few returns to former scenes have.

Nevertheless, those waves of depression that had plagued me in Shaw came from time to time, especially when I thought about the future and my lack of success in finding a husband. A popular expression among my circle of friends was "the quarter century jitters" that came upon single girls at the thought of officially becoming an Old Maid at that point. At twenty-four, I was dangerously close.

One Friday in February, LaNelle and I drove home to the Delta for the weekend, and while I was there my mother gave me some good advice. When I shared with her my problem, she said she thought the perfect person for me was "just around the corner" and that I would find him if I would free myself from my present relationship, that old college attachment that was dragging on and on.

It took about a month for her advice to work its way into my will, but one Sunday afternoon in March I decided the time had come to make a break, and I wrote a letter to that effect. There was such a flood of tears as I wrote that I had to be careful not to let any of them fall on the paper, although I really thought a little tear-smudged ink would be a nice touch. After the letter was mailed, however, I had not the slightest regret. In fact, to my surprise, I experienced the freedom of being perfectly content and happy with life as it was.

Something of significant spiritual import happened when I released that relationship. It meant that I was taking my hands off the problem of finding a mate and trusting God with it. I had to give up my feeble attempts toward a solution in order for Him to move in and do it right. I didn't understand that then, but we are often led through things we don't understand. My mother was right; the right person was just around the corner, and I had just taken the step that would permit the divine Matchmaker to bring us together.

3

Those Whom God Has Joined Together

Easter came late in 1957. By the time I went home for spring break, I had been enjoying tranquillity of soul for several weeks and still had no regrets about terminating a significant friendship that had afforded me a measure of emotional security. I left Dallas by bus on April 13, the day before Palm Sunday. It was an express bus with the nearest stop to Leland at Greenville, ten miles away. As we rode across Arkansas, the driver told me he could let me out on the highway outside of Leland if someone could meet me there. So when we stopped at the town of Crossett, I called my mother and asked her to meet the bus on Highway 82 in front of Sam's Cafe at midnight. Before hanging up, she asked, "Who is Glenn Hyde? He has been ringing the phone off the wall trying to get you."

"Not him again!" I answered. Glenn was a young officer and instructor pilot stationed at Greenville Air Force Base. I had met him two years before at a party celebrating his safe return after bailing out of a T-33 one night near Cedartown, Georgia. He was the life of the party, proudly displaying the ripcord of the parachute that had saved his life, and keeping everyone's glass filled with sparkling burgundy. I thought he was rather cute, if a little egocentric. At one point, he sat down next to me, and after we talked a few minutes he asked me to stand up. I was wearing what we called "little heels", which added about two inches to my height, making me nearly as tall as he. He asked if I had some low-heeled shoes, and when I told him I did, he wanted to know if I would wear them the upcoming Monday night and go out with him. I didn't think that was such a gracious way to ask a girl out, but social life in the Delta was a little dull that summer, so I accepted. I watched as he carefully wrote my name, address, and telephone number in a little black notebook. (I had heard of those little books men are supposed to have, but this was the first time I had seen one.) Monday came and went and I never heard from him. In other words, he stood me up. Aside from my wounded pride, it was no big disappointment, because I wasn't that interested in going out with him, but when he called, out of the blue, the following fall, I wouldn't give him the time of day. After making him go to great lengths to identify himself, I declined to accept a date. Now my mother was telling me he had popped up again, more than a year later. Oh well, I thought, and my mind moved on to more important things.

Glenn's side of the story was very interesting. He told me later that he waked up that Saturday morning with me on his mind. The only problem was that he couldn't remember my name. (Neither did he remember the famous date that never happened.) With the help of his roommate, he finally identified my entry in the little black book and called my parents' house. When he found out I was coming in that night, he offered to meet the bus. I think my mother kept putting him off by saying she didn't know what time the bus was due, and he kept calling back to ask if she had found out the time. He said later he didn't know why he was so persistent. He just knew he had to see me.

That bug had not bitten me, however, and when he called soon after I arrived at home, I put him off. I had brought a stack of material with me and was planning to get some sewing done that week. I didn't want to waste my time going out with one of those "fly boys" from out at the base, and especially with one who had stood me up. But he persevered, and I agreed to go to an "Easter Dance" at the Officers' Club on Saturday. (That's right, an Easter Dance on Holy Saturday.)

The wonderful thing, the absolutely magical, out-of-this-world thing that happened that night took me completely by surprise. I didn't expect anything more out of the evening than a pleasant diversion. I complained about all the trouble it was to find something to wear, since I had not brought a formal home with me. Searching in the attic, I found a blue net and taffeta dress I had worn in a wedding a few years back. Then I had to go to the trouble of finding flat shoes to go with it. The whole thing was a pain. But I got it all together and was putting the finishing touches on my make-up when my sister Corinne came running into the bedroom and announced, "You have a date with a *beautiful* man!" Oh well, I thought, what do little sisters know?

He did look nice in his dress uniform, made formal by a white shirt and black tie (this was in the days before the elegant formal uniform, the mess dress, came out), and the evening commenced on a pleasant note. The Easter dance was not very well attended, and we were one of a handful of couples there. We had dinner, danced a few times to music provided by the juke box, and engaged in light conversation. We were sitting at the table talking when suddenly a wonderful revelation came to me. It was as if something were unveiled that had been hidden from me a moment before, and I realized that this man in my presence was exactly who I had been waiting for. There was something about the way he laughed, the way his collar fit his neck, and a mysterious likeness to my father, along with his total personality, that completely fulfilled my image of manhood. Such delight I experienced in that moment! It didn't rest on his having the same feelings for me. Just the fact of having found him gave me joy unspeakable.

Shortly after my discovery, the bartender came over to tell Glenn he had a telephone call. He was the base flying safety officer, and the word he received was that a T-33 from Greenville had been involved in an accident somewhere in Arkansas. This meant he had to go to work, so I went with him to his office in Base Operations. I watched as he talked to the pilot, gathered information, and made necessary arrangements with professionalism and efficiency, and berated myself for delaying our date until the end of the week. Between phone calls, he walked over to me, gave me a little peck on the lips, and said, "All work and no play makes Glenn a dull boy!" What can I say? I melted.

It was nearly midnight when he finished, so he headed out the main gate toward town, and I thought I would just die if he took me straight home. I didn't have to worry long, because he suggested that we go for coffee at an all-night restaurant. The evening continued to glow until finally time ran out and he had to take me home. I didn't know how he felt about me, but I knew I had to see him again. When he stopped the car, he told me straightforwardly that I was the girl he had been looking for. Just as directly, I told him I had been thinking the same thing about him. To seal his commitment, he took his wings from his uniform and gave them to me.

When I went into the house, my sisters were getting up to go to the Easter sunrise service. I bounced in, announced, to everyone's amazement, that I had found the man I was going to marry, and crawled into the bed just vacated by Rachel. I never went to sleep, though. The adrenaline was pumping too fast for that. Later that morning, the whole family went to church together. We had to sit down at the front, all six of us in the second pew, and I thought to myself that I would remember that day for the rest of my life. I had never been so happy.

That night, Glenn took me to the house on Lake Ferguson where he and his friend, Joe Bravenec, and dog, Jekyll, lived, and I met the household. While we were there, I tried to bare my soul to him about what I considered a less than perfect moral background, but he was not remotely interested, to my great relief. Later, when I heard the wonderful word from Isaiah that says "Though your sins be as scarlet, they shall be as white as snow," I knew exactly what it meant. No longer having to guard my deep dark secrets was like having a heavy load lifted off my back. We made plans to be together in three weeks, when he would fly to Love Field on a cross-country, and I left Monday for Dallas.

My poor roommates thought I was obnoxious. Who likes to be greeted by a gushy, bubbling character who thinks everything is wonderful at seven o'clock in the morning? I was a little hard to take. They expressed their concern often, saying they hoped I didn't get hurt. That thought never occurred to me. If it had, any fears would have been allayed by Glenn's first letter. When it arrived, I knew it was a historic document and planned then to keep it for posterity. For three of the six pages, he gave me his life history up to his present age of twenty-seven, ending by saying

> I have almost for certain made up my mind to make the Air Force a career unless someone comes along to change my mind, and they will have to change it a hell of a lot.

Concerning flying, he wrote

> The most interesting thing I find in the Air Force is flying, and I thoroughly enjoy it. I've been flying airplanes practically all my life, since I was fifteen anyway. It has always held a fascination for me and I really love it. I don't want you to worry about this flying business and the fact that I fly. I might add this little item of wisdom for some consolation: "Flying in itself is not inherently dangerous, but like the sea, is terribly unforgiving of incompetence and negligence."

Next came his commentary on the previous weekend:

> You know, I had a strange feeling last Saturday, before I finally called you for a date, that something really wonderful would happen. I don't have the

slightest idea what it was, do you? Whatever happened, I'm glad and I certainly hope that this thing—affection, infatuation, love or whatever doesn't ever wear out. I can stand it, can you?

He apologized for getting me home so late both nights (although I was just as guilty as he) and promised to be more conscious of the time in the future. Then he added this:

To be perfectly honest I would much rather have you for always. Think maybe this can be arranged? Like I told you, this ole life of a bachelor gets mighty old and unexciting at times and I am definitely ready and interested in finding the ONE and settle down. Marianne, you fit the bill perfectly in every respect. A little early to make definite plans I know, but still it's food for thought, and besides next March you become officially an Old Maid. Now we can't have that happen, can we? *(I must have told him about the quarter century business.)*

He closed by reminding me that he would see me in Dallas on May 11. "I'll be there with bells ringing," he wrote, "and we'll paint the town red, white, orange, and green—How about that?"

When I drove to Love Field to meet him that Friday afternoon, I had my first experience of fear about his flying, entertaining a host of "what if's": What if he should crash on the way? What if I sat there for hours and he didn't arrive? What if I couldn't get any information about him? Happily, those fears proved groundless, and he arrived right on time. This was the first time I had seen him in a flight suit, and I loved the way he looked. When he greeted me with a kiss, I noticed for the first time the little puffs over his eyes that fascinated me for as long as I knew him.

Before he took off for Greenville on Sunday afternoon, we had decided to set a wedding date for sometime before the first of the year (He needed time to save some money). I notified my school district the next day that I would not be returning and moved back to Leland as soon as school was out.

The first weekend after my return, Glenn took me to Georgia to meet his family. They welcomed me with open arms, and from the first I felt like a member of the family. His mother was so glad he had found someone to love. She told of how sad she had felt when he used to drive away from their house to return to his base with just his dog, Jekyll, sitting in the front seat with him. She and I became very close. I met Glenn's sister, Betty Anne, on that first visit. We became like true sisters, and today she is one of the most important people in my life. It is interesting that I thought I was grown then, at the age of twenty-four, and yet it was such an impressionable age. Such a strong bonding took place between Glenn's family and me that they have remained like my own people ever since.

We left LaGrange with the blessings of the Hyde clan and returned to Greenville for what we thought would be a carefree time of courtship and making wedding plans. We had set a date for the day after Thanksgiving, but like many of the plans of mice and men, it was not to come off that way.

One day late in June, Glenn called me from work and announced that he had just received orders, which I found very exciting. Ever since I had found out I would be marrying someone in the Air Force, I had looked forward to living in different places, and now it sounded as if we would be starting our married life in a new place. Then he told me he was being sent on an unaccompanied assignment to Osan Air Force Base, Korea, in October for thirteen months. What a bombshell! There went our plans. There would be no Thanksgiving wedding. There was no question as to what we would do. Glenn said we should get married ASAP, and everyone agreed, including my father. The night Glenn asked him for my hand, we sat for so long waiting for him to get up the nerve that it was well past Daddy's bedtime when he finally brought up the subject. Before he could get into his prepared speech, Daddy interrupted and said, "I think that will be fine." I accused him of being in a hurry to have me off his hands. We moved our wedding date to July 13, two weeks away.

Never was so much done in so little time. My mother and I spent two days shopping in Memphis and Jackson. Friends and relatives had lovely parties for us on the spur of the moment. We ordered rings and chose china, crystal, and silver patterns. Material was purchased and bridesmaids' dresses made for my sisters. (I was still sewing on Rachel's headpiece the morning of the wedding.)

The wedding was a community effort. Since there was no time to send invitations, a long time family friend, Josie Knox Grimes, who was Society Editor for the *Leland Progress,* went through the telephone book and called to invite people. Anyone she may have missed hopefully read the invitation in the church bulletin the Sunday before the wedding, which was set for eleven o'clock Saturday morning in the Methodist Church. Our friend, Jessie Mae Baggett, who owned a flower shop, made the church beautiful as her wedding gift.

I wore my cousin Margaret's wedding dress. Fortunately we were the same size and she had married just two years before. It was perfect—a simple ballerina-length dress with a princess waist and long sculptured sleeves. The men wore uniforms.

My first piano teacher, Anne Crawford, played the organ. It's a good thing she was such a good musician, because I demanded a lot on short notice. I had taken a course in church music the previous summer at the University of Colorado, in which we studied about wedding music, and of course I wanted to apply everything I had learned. Before then, I had thought a wedding was impossible without beginning and ending with the famous marches of Wagner and Mendelssohn. (I mean, how could you have a wedding without "Here comes the bride, big, fat, and wide"?) In my course, I had learned that there were better selections available, so I made a list of my favorite organ pieces and asked Anne to play them before the ceremony. We marched in to "A Mighty Fortress Is Our God." At the rehearsal, the processional music didn't have the brightness I expected. It sounded dead. She was playing it in the key of C. With my youthful audacity, I asked her to play it in D, which, as it turned out, solved the problem. It may seem unreasonable for me to have asked her to change keys, but I knew she could do it. One of her favorite stories was of the time she was accompanying my mother to sing "The Holy City" in the Baptist church when they were young. Mama came in on the wrong note, requiring Anne to transpose the whole song on the spot, which I'm sure she did without a hitch. My cousin, Lois Bell, sang Burleigh's "O Perfect Love", a copy of which I gave her ten days before the wedding. She sang it in her usual lovely manner, but she surely would have preferred to sing a familiar song.

The ceremony was conducted by Reverend Dorsey Allen, whom I had known since I was a fourth grader at the Methodist camp at Castalian Springs and he was a counselor. In contrast to the nightmares I had of no one showing up for the wedding, the church was full.

Many people contributed to make the reception the festive occasion it was. The Garden Club house was decorated beautifully, featuring my grandmother's cutwork tablecloth on the main table. We cut the cake with a sword to carry out the military theme. The gathering was a small town happening, with much camaraderie and good food. A little reluctantly I broke away from the party to change into my going-away outfit, and we left for a wedding trip to the Mississippi coast and New Orleans.

It had happened. God had heard those prayers prayed in the piano room in the Shaw School and had answered them exceeding abundantly above all that I asked or thought. This was not a time for reflection, so I didn't give Him credit then. That would come later.

4

Boundless Realms of Joy

> *Then surely thou shalt know
> what boundless realms of joy
> the Lord has given us.*[1]

The line quoted above is sung by Adam to Eve in one of my favorite pieces of music, Haydn's oratorio, *The Creation,* based on a text from the book of Genesis and from Milton's *Paradise Lost.* In the third part, after a stirring duet and chorus of praise to God for His creation, Adam and Eve turn their attention to each other. What follows is the most tender of all

---

1. Joseph Haydn, *The Creation in a New Translation by Robert Shaw and Alice Parker* (New York: Lawson-Gould Music Publishers, 1957), p. 132.

love songs. It fairly drips with innocence, devotion, and delight. These are the opening lines:

> *Adam:* Sweet companion!
>   Here beside thee softly fly the golden hours.
>   Every moment is rapture
>   Naught of sadness lingers near.
>
> *Eve:* Dearest husband! Here beside thee,
>   Floods of joy o'erflow my heart
>   That thou love me is my blessing,
>   Thine forever is my life.[2]

To compose this beautiful duet, Haydn must have known something of the tender love that can flow between a man and a woman. How he learned is a mystery, because his biographers report that he was married to a shrew; but the music to which he set the adoring words of this passage gives a vivid picture and exquisite feeling of the first of all human loves. It shows, I think, what God had in mind when he invented the institution of marriage.

The quality of that love duet is the same quality that pervaded the blissful early weeks of marriage for Glenn and me. We were allowed to experience a little taste of heaven on earth, until the dark cloud of his impending departure loomed too near for happiness to continue.

The trusty dog, Jekyll, an exceptional blending of beagle and bird dog, was waiting for us at home when we returned from our honeymoon. Joe, Glenn's former roommate, had taken a room at my Aunt Bessie's house, leaving the house on Lake Ferguson for us, where we lived for the next two months. It was an idyllic setting, with a view that took in a bend in that former segment of the Mississippi River. The house was a rustic two-

---

2 Ibid., pp. 133-136.

story cement structure built for weekends and vacations without all the comforts of home. On the ground floor was one breezy screened-in room and some showers. Upstairs were bedrooms, a living room, and a kitchen. We set up a sitting area downstairs with lawn furniture, and I spent most of my days there writing thank-you notes and planning meals. We entertained a lot, using our new Pink Vista dishes and treasured Chantilly silverware.

Glenn had a motorboat, and we spent much time during long summer evenings and weekends on the lake. He liked to water ski, but I, being disgracefully non-athletic, preferred to stay in the boat. When we rode on the lake, Jekyll would fix himself on the bow like a sentinel, and no matter how fast we went, he never budged from his spot. Glenn also had a little sailfish he had built, using a piece of parachute for a sail. We took it out often, spending more time off of it than on.

The summer was like a long vacation, although Glenn did go to work. One afternoon, he called and told me he would probably have to work all night because a jet trainer had just crashed, so I went to Leland to spend the night. He joined me there in the small hours of the morning and said two men had died in the crash. He told me some of the details of the scene he came upon, as a member of the rescue team, in terms that seemed almost callous. I felt all the pain that the shield of his professionalism would not allow him to feel and thought I simply could not bear it if something like that should happen to him.

The slight change in the air in September that signaled the approach of autumn also signaled the end of our Eden-like days on the lake. After having our household goods packed and stored, we visited his family in Georgia. One evening shortly before the end of our stay there, while he and I and his parents were sitting in the living room, he told them how much he appreciated the heritage they had given him and thanked them for it. It didn't take much during those days to bring tears to his mother's and my eyes, and this was one time they flowed. The morning we left, he got up early, while it was still dark, to tell his father good-bye before he went to work. When he came back to bed, he cried, saying he didn't think he would ever see his dad alive again. Mr. Hyde is now eighty-five years old and, as he puts it, doesn't even take any pills. So many things we worry about never happen.

The dreaded moment of farewell arrived for me on October 14. (The fact that I remember the date after all these years reveals something of the emotional weight I felt.) We drove to Memphis the day before and stayed at the Peabody Hotel. That night we went up on the Peabody roof, the Skyway, to have a little celebration, but it was hardly that. I have a matchbook picture taken of us that night that shows a pitifully forlorn pair. When I left the Memphis airport the next day after watching his plane take off for San Francisco, I was so bereft I cried nearly all the way back to Leland. The days that followed were unbearably sad. I felt as if my very heart had been torn out, and could burst into tears at the drop of a hat. The pain was made even worse by the fact that no one could understand how miserable I was. The sorrow of something as benign as separation is not something other people recognize. Even though my heart was broken, I was expected to be as strong as usual and act normal.

I quickly settled into a routine, teaching a class of piano students at the school, which kept me busy during the week. I lived for letters from Korea, which usually arrived two or three at a time. After Christmas, which was an especially difficult time, I told my mother

I was glad the holidays were over so I could start "knocking off January", an attitude exactly opposite St. Paul's admonition to redeem the time. I hated that year, but seen in the context of my whole life, I believe it was necessary. There was something essential that I needed to learn before Glenn and I really began our life together. I had to learn to place my security in God, not in my husband.

One day in May, I was in the school auditorium playing "Land of Hope and Glory" for a graduation rehearsal when a friend and fellow music student from L. S. U., Carolyn Thornton, walked in. For the past year, she had worked with a group called Moral Re-Armament (MRA). While we visited, she asked me to drive with her to the American headquarters of MRA at Mackinac Island, Michigan, for a conference early in June. With an uneventful summer stretching out before me, a trip to the Great Lakes sounded good and I agreed to go.

Moral Re-Armament, as its name implies, operated on the premise that the problems we faced in the world were caused by a moral decline and that the solution lay in returning to God and embracing absolute moral standards. Developments in our culture in the thirty years since I was introduced to the movement have surely borne out the truth of that assessment. My contact with Moral Re-Armament gave me a historical view of contemporary culture and left me with a permanently implanted consciousness of the choice each of us faces, to be part of the problem or part of the solution.

I was also deeply impressed with the quality of life of the people I met at Mackinac Island. Everyone had a story to tell about how God had worked in his or her life, often in very specific, circumstantial ways, and always bringing reconciliation and wholeness. The occasion of this particular gathering was the celebration of the eightieth birthday of the founder of the movement, Dr. Frank Buchman, and people came from every corner of the world. Many speeches were made from the platform, but the things I remember are those that I heard during conversations over meals. Hardly a meal went by without someone at the table telling his story. The effect of this was the feeding and strengthening of my little mustard seed of faith. I knew that I was walking on thin ice with my happiness and security totally dependent on my husband, and I wanted more than anything in the world to have the kind of bedrock security these people seemed to have. The stories left no doubt that it came from God.

At the end of the week I had planned to be there, I decided to stay for the remainder of the conference, serving tables in the dining room as my contribution to the work. By the end of the summer, after being immersed in a community of people who sought to be guided by God, I knew that God was real and that he was active in the lives of those who sought Him, and I could see that He had indeed worked in my life in some rather dramatic ways before I was aware of it. I left Mackinac Island determined to live my life for God, come what may. I had much to learn about the Christian faith before I would be able to do this with any degree of consistency, but the foundation had been laid.

Glenn received orders to report to Laughlin Air Force Base in Del Rio, Texas, which pleased me immensely. I didn't know anything about Del Rio, but since it was Texas it had to be good. After a joyful reunion in November and a month spent visiting relatives in Georgia and Mississippi, we drove to the southwest Texas town made famous by a high- powered radio station across the Rio Grande in Mexico.

Laughlin was a Strategic Air Command base, the home of the 4080th Strategic Wing, devoted to the mission of the super-secret U-2 reconnaissance aircraft. It was the strangest airplane we had ever seen, and he had seen many more than I. It had very long wings and took off at such a steep angle it seemed to shoot nearly straight up. When it came in for a landing, it made a shrill, whining sound.

Glenn was not happy being at a SAC base, having just come from a fighter squadron in Korea and being a fighter pilot at heart, but if he had to be there, he did want to be involved with the primary business of the base. His orders indicated that he was being assigned to the base as a T-33 instructor pilot. He was evidently an outstanding instructor. I have among his papers several letters written by senior officers who came to Laughlin to be checked out in the T-bird commending him for his excellent ability in that area. Still, he did not want to spend his Air Force career instructing. As he put it, "If I'm going to be in this business, I want to be on the first team." From the time of his arrival at Laughlin, he set out to find out all he could about the mission of the base and the weird airplane they flew. This was no easy task in 1958, as the U-2 program was carried on under a heavy cloak of secrecy.

In the meantime, things were happier at home. We rented a little concrete block duplex on West Tenth Street, and I couldn't have been more pleased if it had been a castle. On one trip to San Antonio, we bought furniture for it, delighting in each piece. I plunged into housekeeping with fervor, studying cookbooks, making shopping lists, cooking elaborate meals, relishing trips to the Laundromat, and cleaning house every day. (Is that not fervor?) Among our purchases was the first television set for each of us, and we spent the winter evenings watching original broadcasts of shows that have become classics. My favorite was Bob Cummings on Tuesday night and he liked Perry Mason on Saturday. Mrs. Hyde had taught me how to crochet granny squares, and I busied myself making them while we watched. Glenn was fascinated and had me teach him how to crochet. We sat and crocheted together many evenings, and I have today a pink afghan made from those squares. I also spent time sewing. I had bought a little Singer Featherweight sewing machine while he was in Korea, and it was one of the joys of my life. I could set it up anywhere, but my favorite place was on the coffee table. I sat on the sofa and used it, making some lovely dresses from material brought from the Far East. Those were precious days.

We started immediately to visit churches. The one we chose was the First Baptist Church. I was happy to be baptized and duly received into membership. I think I had secretly wanted to be a Baptist since resisting those altar calls at the Leland Baptist Church.

We hardly got involved in the life of the church, however, before we left town for several months. Glenn went to Maxwell Air Force Base in Alabama to take a course called Squadron Officers School (SOS). It was there that I met two young women who would become my closest of friends and would remain so through the years. Helen Doering and Mary Nell Sala were wives of two U-2 pilots from Laughlin who were going through SOS. We met under the worst of circumstances, at least from my point of view.

I arrived in Montgomery several weeks into our tour of duty there, having remained in Del Rio to finish the school year for a teacher who had resigned due to pregnancy. Glenn flew to Del Rio and we made the long drive back to Alabama non-stop in our brand new non-air-conditioned station wagon. I was miserable the whole trip with the heat and with a nausea akin to motion sickness always just below the surface. When we arrived at our non-air-conditioned apartment in Montgomery, I found that I had suddenly lost my appetite for coffee, without which I had previously been unable to function, and was totally devoid of energy or motivation to accomplish the slightest task. We soon realized that I must be pregnant and were overjoyed. We both wanted children.

When I think of that summer, the scene that comes to mind is one of me lying around the apartment all day in front of fans and eating crackers. We ate out nearly every night, usually at a place where I could get shrimp and melon, the only foods that appealed to me. Somehow in the midst of that, I established a friendship with Mary Nell and Helen. They understood and accepted my lethargic and somewhat anti-social attitude. Helen was expecting her first child, Christopher, who would be born in November, and although she felt good at that point, she remembered how it had been at the beginning. They were eager to welcome me to Montgomery, and one morning soon after I arrived, they called at 7:00 o'clock to invite me to play golf with them. I thought that was ludicrous. I wouldn't play golf even if I felt like it (remember, I'm a non-athlete), and certainly not first thing in the morning. But we did manage to do things together at more civilized hours of the day and became very well acquainted. Today, not one of us is married to one of the men who brought us together and we live miles apart, but whenever a vital event occurs, such as a birth, death, marriage, or divorce, we are in contact with each other. I saw a piece of needlework recently that said "friends are flowers in the garden of life" and thought of Mary Nell and Helen.

Mary Nell was with me later in Del Rio when I received the distressing news from my doctor that my pregnancy was not progressing normally and that I would probably miscarry. I did lose the baby in November while I was visiting my family in Mississippi, and it was a terrible blow. The weekend after it happened, Glenn flew over to see me, and he was wonderful, listening as I shared all the bitter details of the ordeal and letting me grieve. It's hard for people who have not been through this kind of experience to know how to care for someone during such a time. One thing that did not help was to be reminded that I could just have another baby. Of course I planned to have another baby, but first I had to grieve for the one I had just lost. My friend, Catherine Benson, pointed this out to me when she said, "You don't want another baby, you want *this* baby, don't you?" She was right.

The sorrow did not go away quickly, but I was soon distracted from it by the fact that the long-awaited housing on base was nearing completion and we would soon be moving into a brand new home. Because our husbands were close in date of rank, Mary Nell and I received calls at about the same time to choose our houses. We went to the Housing Office on base soon after my return to Del Rio and studied maps and house plans. We each decided on a house, a duplex actually, on Lawhon Street and were told by the sergeant in charge that the houses were ready except for "picture frames" (toilet seats). Glenn and I moved into our quarters, with picture frames by then installed, over the Thanksgiving weekend. For the first time we had space to unpack all our wedding presents. There was no shortage of dishes, but the house was glaringly sparse in furnishings. The adventure of rectifying that deficiency would come later; for the time being, we were content with our home.

In December, Lieutenant Hyde became Captain Hyde, and we celebrated pinning on his bars at the New Year's Eve party at the Officers' Club. He was gorgeous in his new mess dress uniform, and I felt elegant in a brocade dress I had made from material from Japan. He spent the evening ordering champagne for everyone in sight. We were young and in love and the world was our apple. I still had not found the firm place to stand that I knew I had to have, but that discovery would not be far into the future.

5

Peering Over the Edge of Eternity

With the beginning of the year 1960 I embarked upon one of the most colorful and happy periods of my life—one that left deep, inordinately detailed traces in my memory. We lived in the house on Lawhon Street for three and a half years. The warm, sunny days that made their appearance in southwest Texas in late winter, giving a foretaste of spring, drew my attention to gardening. We made flower beds in every available spot, and I planted roses, bulbs, and thousands of seeds. Mary Nell and I conferred constantly about our gardens, calling each other to come and look every time a seedling popped its head out of the soil or a dormant rose stalk put out a bud. We did not bother Helen with such trivia, as she had more pressing concerns with a new baby to care for.

Later, Helen and I spent a lot of time together working on two-piano music. We were invited to join the Del Rio Music Club, which was a lovely organization of ladies that met monthly for musical programs presented by members. Meetings were held in an old stone building near the railroad track off Highway 90 at 4 o'clock in the afternoon. A train was scheduled to come by shortly thereafter, causing every program to have to come to a grinding halt while it thundered by. Helen and I participated in many of those programs.

One summer, a program was given on base by a chorus of officers' wives, who sang, among other things, selections from *Camelot*. (I find that a poignant memory in light of subsequent national events. As we sang words that reminded us never to forget that "once there was a spot for a brief, shining moment known as Camelot," we were waltzing through a political era later to be likened to the mythical Camelot by its first lady. In an interview with journalist Teddy White just hours after President Kennedy was assassinated, Mrs. Kennedy placed this epitaph on his administration.) Helen and I were asked to provide two-piano music for the second half of the program. The San Antonio Music Company was generous enough to provide two Steinway grand pianos for our performance. We worked our heads off, having much fun in the process.

We practiced at my house, where, through the kindness of the above-mentioned company, I had two pianos. One of the first purchases Glenn and I made for the new house was a piano, and I started a class of piano students to help pay for the instrument. The piano salesman from the San Antonio Music Company came to Del Rio regularly, driving a van loaded with new pianos, and always stopped by to find out if I knew of anyone who was interested in buying one. Many times I did. On one of those visits, I mentioned that I liked my piano, but that the one I really wanted was a Steinway. He took out his pencil, did some figuring, and offered to trade my piano for the one I wanted for a surprisingly small amount of cash, forfeiting his commission I fear. I couldn't resist and agreed to the deal. When he delivered the elegant *Louis XV* console to my house, he asked if he could leave the original piano in case someone in the area wanted to buy it. That's how I got two pianos and, incidentally, got the long blank wall in my living room furnished. I had to call them to come and get their piano the week before we moved three years later.

The piano transaction occurred at a time when Glenn was in Waco for several weeks. The next time he came home after the second piano arrived, he surprised me by driving up in an eight-year-old black Plymouth sedan he had picked up for a song in Waco. (I should point out that back in those days it was unusual for one family to have two cars.) Later he and George Bull would have a grand time overhauling the engine. After he had it reupholstered and painted white, he boasted that he had a brand new 1953 Plymouth (in 1962, which was a novelty, as we didn't drive cars for so many years back then). It was a very good car. My sister Rachel eventually traded it in on the first car she purchased.

On the same weekend—that of the piano and the car—we acquired a new dog. Our dog, Jekyll, had sired a litter of puppies down the street, and one of them was the image of her father. We laid claim to that one, planning to give her to a couple of Jekyll-lovers in Leland. When we brought the puppy home, Glenn announced that he had two pianos, two cars, and two dogs, and that the next thing he was going to get was two wives. (Fortunately, he never got around to that.)

The first opening of a school year after we moved on base found me back in the classroom. There was such a teacher shortage that the Del Rio Independent School District hired me on an emergency certificate to teach first grade. I took the job, not for the money, although we could surely use it, but because I thought I would be more likely to get pregnant again if my mind were taken up with something as consuming as teaching. I was wrong about that, but I loved the teaching. An experienced teacher at East Side School took me under her wing and taught me enough to look as if I knew what I was doing, and I taught there for three years, until we left Del Rio.

It was hard for me to realize that the pleasant life style we had in Del Rio was not permanent. Glenn kept reminding me, especially when I got carried away with projects having to do with the house, that we would be moving on one day. I didn't like to think about that. I remember one late winter afternoon driving home on Highway 277 from a Music Club meeting pondering the fact that this whole busy framework of life that I loved so much couldn't last.

During the course of those happy years, my attitude toward Glenn's flying underwent a transformation from extreme apprehension to release. At first, I was in a nervous fit every time he took off in an airplane. Any time he was due home after flying, I would keep looking down the street to see if the base chaplain's car was still in his driveway. Once I imagined him knocking on my door to tell me Glenn had crashed, and I thought that my reaction would be to slam the door in his face and run. I simply could not face the possibility of losing him. But during the many hours I spent alone I began to change. I used to think that thoughts were just thoughts, with origins no further away than one's subconscious. I now believe that more of our thought life than we realize, especially for those whose spiritual channel is open, comes from the Holy Spirit or from the adversary. A comparison of thoughts with the Word of God can reveal which of the sources generates them. I believe the Holy Spirit worked through my thought life to guide me through the great problem of fear over Glenn's flying.

One day I was preparing supper on my gray kitchen countertop, expecting Glenn home from flying at any moment, and I thought how stupid it was of me to ruin this beautiful time we had together by allowing myself to get worked up to a state of nervous exhaustion and ending up welcoming him home as if from the dead. And I thought, as terrible as it would be if the worst should happen, that God could handle even that for me; it would not be the end of everything. So I decided right then to cool it on worrying. That, of course, was easier said than done, but the decision took a lot of pressure off our marriage and was a step toward my gaining victory in the matter.

I was far from free of worry, though. When I got home from school, I used to go immediately to his closet and check to see if his flying boots were there. If they were, I was happy; if not, I got that little lump in my throat that worry brings. One day it occurred to me that the days when he flew were the days he loved. He considered the days he went to work without flying to be bad days. What kind of wife was I if I was happy when he was unhappy and sad when he was happy? I realized that I had it all backwards, and I decided to be happy at the right times. My emotions did not always cooperate, but being committed in my will to this new way of looking at things carried me further down the road to true release and it surely enhanced our marriage. (St. Paul told us to rejoice with those who rejoice and weep with those who weep, so I was right on track, but I didn't know that then.)

The more Glenn found out about the U-2 program, the more he wanted to get into it. After he had knocked on doors and pulled strings until he could think of nothing else to do, we prayed about it. (When all else fails, follow directions.) It was most unusual for us to pray together, so I know he must really have wanted the assignment. One afternoon we knelt beside our bed and asked God to open the way for him to be assigned to the 4028th Strategic Reconnaissance Squadron if it were His will. In September of 1960, he received the much desired transfer, and on October 19 he took his first flight in that strange-looking airplane with the long wings, a U-2. Since the plane flown at Laughlin had just one seat, his first flight was also his solo flight. It was a big event. The principal of my school, Mr. Brown, came over to my room at about 11 o'clock that morning and told me Glenn had just called to say he was back on the ground. We celebrated that night.

Although there had been a number of U-2 crashes in the early days of the program, no plane had been lost since we had been at Laughlin, and I was amazingly undisturbed by his long flights into the stratosphere. (The altitude at which they flew was classified, but it was known to be high.) Then one Friday afternoon in March of 1962, I walked into my house from work to the ringing of the telephone. It was my friend Helen calling to tell me that John Campbell was missing on a flight in California. He and his wife, Amy, were our back door neighbors and were good friends. I went to their house and found many other wives already there. The men in the squadron and their wives were a close-knit group, so it was almost like being with family. I found out that John and another pilot, Rudy Anderson, had been on a special assignment in California and John had disappeared on a flight the night before. Jane Anderson was one of the women at Amy's house. They had been there most of the day, so that night I volunteered to spend the night, since Glenn was on a cross-country and I had no little ones at home to care for. It was one of the darkest nights I ever spent. At a time like that one thinks a lot about the fragility of this earthly life and about eternity. I thought of myself going through an ordeal like the one facing Amy. The next morning the house was again filled with friends and I went to town to keep a beauty shop appointment. Before heading back to the base, I called the Campbell house and received the sad news that John had gone down with his plane. A dark cloud of sorrow settled over the base at the loss of one of our own.

The work of the 4028th was carried on from Laughlin as well as from locations all over the globe. During the time Glenn participated he had assignments of from two to three months in Alaska, Panama, and Australia. He served his tour of duty "down under" in 1962 during the fall. Although I missed him when he was gone, my life was structured around my own business, and I had lots of human contact at work and with my neighbors on base. News spread freely through the community, and we stayed well-informed on all matters of an unclassified nature.

One weekend in October, I heard talk of two of our men being off on a special assignment that sounded unusual. Then on Monday afternoon, October 22, I switched on the television and saw President Kennedy announcing that offensive missile sites had been discovered in Communist Cuba. He proceeded to explain that we had incontrovertible evidence that some of these installations included medium-range ballistic missiles capable of carrying a nuclear warhead for a distance of more than one thousand nautical miles. In addition, sites not yet completed appeared to be designed for intermediate-range ballistic missiles that could travel twice as far. A quick mental calculation told me that most of the hemisphere was vulnerable to attack from the little island just ninety miles from our shores. As my mind was working to process this startling news, the light dawned and I suddenly knew that the "evidence" to which he was referring included pictures taken by our pilots, Steve Heyser and Rudy Anderson. The President emphasized in his speech that this secret, sudden, and substantial build-up of strategic armaments by the Soviet Union could not be tolerated, and he outlined the steps he was ordering for a resolution of the situation. [1]

For the next thirteen days, those of us at Laughlin were intensely aware of the crisis. In addition to the fact that the nation stood poised at the brink of a nuclear showdown with the Soviet Union, nine more pilots from Laughlin had joined Heyser and Anderson at their operation location in Florida to help carry out the President's orders for "continued and increased close surveillance of Cuba and its military build-up." He also ordered a naval blockade, euphemistically called a quarantine, of the island to prevent any additional shipment of offensive military equipment. Any confrontation on the sea could trigger the unthinkable war.

In a televised session of the United Nations Security Council, our ambassador to that body, Adlai Stevenson, dramatically challenged Soviet Ambassador V. A. Zorin to admit that the weapons in question existed. When the Russian stalled, Stevenson replied in his now-

---

[1] I was helped in reconstructing these details by reading Robert Kennedy's memoir of the Cuban crisis, *Thirteen Days* (New York: W. W. Norton, 1969).

famous statement that he was prepared to wait for an answer "until hell freezes over", and then presented the photographs of the Russian armaments.

On Saturday, October 27, a plane flown by Anderson went down over Cuba, presumably shot down. In the hours that followed, the flurry of communication already underway between Washington and Moscow continued and the White House struggled to solve the crisis without plunging the world into irrevocable tragedy. Then a message came from Soviet Chairman Nikita Khrushchev that Russia would dismantle and withdraw the missiles under adequate supervision and inspection.

All the while, we at Laughlin hoped, prayed and wondered about the fate of Rudy Anderson. Had he been able to escape from his ill-fated plane alive, as Frank Powers had when his U-2 was shot down over Russia three years before? Or did he go down with his plane as John Campbell had in California earlier that year? A number of days passed before we knew. United Nations Secretary General U Thant traveled to Cuba as the crisis was winding down, and upon his return told reporters at the airport in New York that the Cubans had agreed to return Major Anderson's body. That's how we knew he was dead. When I heard the live broadcast, I ran out my kitchen door to the sidewalk in back, where several of us gathered to share our shock and grief. The country returned to business-as-usual, and Laughlin mourned.

Glenn could hardly stand to be in Australia sitting out the action. He came home in December and marched right in to request that he be put on the Cuban project, which was becoming an on-going thing and was operating out of Laughlin by this time, instead of Florida. Later, on the day after Christmas, our station wagon was packed with borrowed camping gear and we were about to leave for a few days on a deer lease on a neighboring ranch when the phone rang. Glenn got his wish. They wanted him to report to work right away to be briefed for a flight to the Caribbean. He changed clothes and went to work and I went around returning tents, stoves, and sleeping bags.

Take-off for the flights to Cuba was in the early morning, which necessitated retiring very early the evening before. The telephone rang at two or three o'clock to call the pilot to work. The routine was invigorating for Glenn. He sprang out of bed and was dressed and out of there in no time, leaving me at loose ends. It helped a lot when I discovered a radio station from Dallas that played classical music in the middle of the night. I would put my mind to work following the structure of the music I heard, usually dropping off to sleep in the middle of some development section.

Once Glenn was scheduled to fly and dutifully went to bed at the appointed hour only to wake up after sunrise, having received no wake-up call. He panicked and called the squadron, asking "what the hell happened" and complaining of bedsores. The mission had been canceled by the Department of Defense during the night. He was scheduled for a flight the day after New Year's Day in 1963. We watched the news the night before and saw a Cuban New Year's parade, including military hardware that Castro claimed could keep Cuban skies free of intruders. It was awesome to hear that and know that my husband was going to be one of those "intruders" the next day. He returned safely from that flight and from all that he flew in the early weeks of 1963, earning a Distinguished Flying Cross for one of them.

During those days I lived in two worlds—the familiar earthly, mortal world and the unseen world of eternity and immortality. On the mornings that Glenn flew I went the long way to work through the main gate to Highway 90, which took me past the squadron. I saw his little white Plymouth there and thought of the possibility that he might never drive it home again; he could cross the line over into eternity any day. (I failed to remember that the same was true for all of us.) At about that time, the base commissary started carrying McCormick spices in those fancy bottles that are familiar today but were special then, and spice racks could be ordered to hold them. One night after Glenn had gone to bed, I filled out an order for one. It still holds spices in my kitchen, and every time I notice it, I think the phrase "peering over the edge of eternity." That's what I was doing when I got it.

Our church home after we moved on base became the base chapel, where I directed the choir for a while. One of the friends I made there was Gladys Ringdahl, the wife of a chaplain who was close to retirement. She was a dear Christian and became somewhat of a mentor to me. During my "eternity peering" days, she gave me a copy of a book called *Beyond Our Selves* by Catherine Marshall. I had thought of Catherine Marshall from time to time since her earlier book, *A Man Called Peter*, had made such an impression on me back in college. and I had seen a copy of a later of book of hers, *To Live Again*, in the base library one day when I was scanning the biography section. I was glad to learn from the title that she had managed to rebuild her life after her husband's death, but for some reason I was not interested in reading about it then. I did, however, make a mental note of the book's existence.

I was, on the other hand, very interested in reading *Beyond Our Selves* and from the moment I opened it could hardly put it down. Each chapter explored a spiritual principle that was illustrated with moving accounts of real people who had experienced those principles in their lives. It reinforced what I had learned at Mackinac Island, that God is a real God who honors a commitment to Him by working in specific and good ways in one's life. I read and reread the book, especially the chapter called "The Prayer of Relinquishment". In that chapter, the author pointed out that fear is evil because in God's eyes it is acting out a lack of trust in Him. The first step to answered prayer, she said, is to walk right up to the thing feared most and admit to its possibility, remembering that God and His power are still the supreme reality. She explained this as the ultimate prayer of faith in a way that made perfect sense to me. The prayer of faith is not believing some specific thing with never a doubt, like, for instance, believing that Glenn would always be safe when he flew; rather the real prayer of faith is the one that says "O.K., Lord, you've got him; do with him as you will and I trust you no matter what." That is faith in action. She concluded the explanation with these encouraging words: "...the act of placing what we cherish most in His hands is to Him the sweet music of the essence of faith."[2] There was the answer to the fear that was coloring my whole life.

When I prayed the Prayer of Relinquishment, I was not playing games with God; it was not some kind of manipulative ploy to get my way. I knew that in this broken world bad things happen. I had just read *Through Gates of Splendor*, Elisabeth Elliot's account of the death of her husband, Jim, and four other missionaries at the hands of Auca Indians in Equador. If God didn't protect those men, then surely my relinquishing Glenn wouldn't guarantee his protection. His ways are beyond my knowing, but I did know that when I put Glenn completely in His hands I was giving Him

---

[2] Catherine Marshall, *Beyond Our Selves* (New York: McGraw-Hill, 1961), p. 88.

permission to protect or withhold protection. It was like a wrenching to contemplate tearing myself away from Glenn and giving him to God. I wondered at the time why that was, since I really had no control anyway. As I write about this now, I wonder if perhaps I did have more control than I knew. It is a known fact of Christianity that God wants His people involved with Him in His work. This is borne out by the fact that we are encouraged throughout scripture to pray. If God wanted to run the earthly show single-handedly, like a giant chess game, there would be no need for prayer—certainly not for prayers of petition. And if He takes our prayers seriously, we need to be very careful about what we pray for. Psalm 106 has some sobering words for those of us who would participate through prayer, when it says, about the children of Israel, "He gave them their request, but sent leanness to their soul." I wanted to be sure my requests were in line with His will, and I knew the only way was to withhold nothing from Him. The Holy Spirit was urging me to pray the Prayer of Relinquishment, and one day I knelt beside my bed and laid the most precious thing in my life, my husband, on the altar. Afterward, there was peace, like having lost a heavy load. Someone much more capable than I was in charge now and I was free. That doesn't mean I never got that automatic lump in my throat and sick feeling in the pit of my stomach when I thought Glenn was overdue from a flight. Long-standing emotional habits don't change overnight. But underneath it all, I knew everything was under control. It made the months that followed the best Glenn and I ever spent together.

Those months came and went, each with its own disappointment that the baby we wanted so much was not on the way. We went through the testing routine to determine if there was a physical problem, but none was found. Then we met a couple who had just adopted a darling little redheaded boy and they told us about the place in Houston through which they got him. We decided to try to adopt a child and contacted the agency, called Homes of St. Mark. After the forms were completed and letters of reference sent in, we drove to Houston on Valentine's Day in 1963 for an interview at the agency's house on North Braeswood. We were told that we would hear from them as soon as an appropriate child became available, and we went back to Del Rio to await a much anticipated telephone call.

As it turned out, the days at Del Rio were numbered. Plans were announced to transfer the 4080th Wing to Davis-Monthan AFB in Arizona that summer. Laughlin was to become a training base. At the same time, Glenn's turn came for a three-month temporary duty at Eielson AFB, Alaska, beginning the first of June. We decided to move out of our house early and spend the summer together in Alaska before moving to Tucson. I resigned from my job three weeks before the end of school, and we left Del Rio on May 10, pulling a 17-foot travel trailer. Although it was exciting to be off on such an adventure, I hated leaving Del Rio. Before we left town, Glenn's name above the door of our house had been replaced by that of the next occupant and it really upset me. How could they so quickly give away my house! Glenn had been trying to convince me for three years that it was not my house, but somehow it never got through my thick head. I grieved over leaving.

The trip to Alaska was an experience to be remembered. We drove through Tucson to look over our new base, then headed north, with stops at the Grand Canyon, Salt Lake City, Yellowstone, and other sites of magnificence. We experienced much camaraderie with fellow travelers along the Alaska highway, especially during the numerous breakdowns of our station wagon.

On one of our unscheduled delays, I sat in the trailer and read *The Agony and the Ecstasy* while the snow fell outside and Glenn worked all night in the garage next door helping the mechanic replace broken valve springs. By the time we rolled into Fairbanks, at the zero hour, we were sick of traveling and wished we could move into a real building that included a bathtub. Instead, we pulled our dirty, travel-worn trailer into a mobile home park just outside the main gate of Eielson and hooked up for the summer.

On one leg of our trip on the Alaska highway, we forgot to secure the kitchen cabinet doors. When we opened up that night we were greeted by a mess of dishes (plastic, fortunately) and groceries all over the place. It all got cleaned up except some instant coffee that had spilled in one of the cabinets. The more I tried to sponge it out, the worse it seemed to become. Soon after we parked for the summer, I began to be acutely aware of the smell of coffee and it made me sick. At the same time I lost my energy and motivation. Even though the smell in the trailer was most unpleasant, I stayed there nearly all the time, lying down doing nothing. I was miserable until it occurred to both of us that, joy of all joys, I might be pregnant! That indeed was the case, but Glenn lost his partner in adventure at that point. I was no more fun. Everything I did was with much effort and little enthusiasm, but he was a sport and put up with me. I was desperate about keeping this baby. I remember thinking one afternoon as I lay on the piece of foam rubber supported by plywood that was our bed that I just could not face the disappointment of losing it.

Because a drive back to Tucson could have threatened my pregnancy, we decided to sell our car and trailer in Alaska and fly back. I left Fairbanks one night two weeks before the end of Glenn's assignment at Eielson on Alaska Airlines and arrived in Memphis the following afternoon. My sister Rachel and my mother met me and we spent the night at the Holiday Inn before driving to Leland. I'll never forget how luxurious it felt to be in a "real" room with real beds, a real bathroom, and carpet on the floor. I was ready for some creature comforts, more of which awaited me in Mississippi. We went there after I had the joy of seeing my first nephew, one-month-old Nathan Bradford, who lived in Memphis.

By the time I flew to Tucson in September, the difficult early months of my pregnancy had passed and I felt like my old self again. The Sunday afternoon that I landed at the Tucson airport I saw Glenn standing in the covered outside concourse, and he looked so bright and happy. I had never seen such a look on his face. I remember thinking that I didn't know he cared so much about me.

We had a good time greeting old friends and visiting them in their new houses. We rented a little white house with clerestory windows and a fireplace, novelties for us, on East Julia Street and had fun setting up housekeeping again. I located an obstetrician, who told me I should be able to have a baby like falling off a log. Glenn and I drove by the hospital one Sunday afternoon and talked of my having the baby there in March. Our new framework was taking shape.

Then he learned that he was scheduled for the Cuban detachment, which was now operated out of Barksdale AFB in Louisiana, in the spring. We discussed it and decided that if he could get his assignment changed to the fall, it would be better. Then he would be at home when the baby came. He was able to do that, so after just three weeks in our new place, we packed up our new air-conditioned (!)

Oldsmobile and made the long drive to Mississippi, where I would stay while he was at Barksdale.

On the first night, we stayed in El Paso. The baby was just beginning to make his presence known. That night, while we were sitting up in bed reading, I felt a vigorous kick and told Glenn about it. He looked over at me with a thoughtful, smiling expression and said, "It's nice, isn't it?" We were really together. The next night we stayed in Del Rio. How strange it felt to be in a motel in Del Rio. I was sad. It was a painful "going back". The third night was in College Station, where we saw my father's alma mater, Texas A & M. I had no idea then that those hallowed grounds would be home for four years for the child I was carrying and that I would become as caught up as he in the inexplicable Aggie Spirit.

Finally, I was deposited at Leland. We saw each other again the first weekend in November, when he met my mother and me in Jackson to share homecoming at Millsaps with Rachel. At the football game, he gave Mama and me a running commentary, explaining everything Rachel's boy friend, Rocky, the Millsaps fullback, did. Rocky is now my brother-in-law. On Sunday we all went to church at Galloway Memorial Methodist Church, where my mother's friend since childhood, Dr. Jeff Cunningham, was minister. It was a happy weekend.

The following Saturday night my mother and I returned from an outing to find, to my delight, our white Oldsmobile parked in the driveway. Glenn was inside so sound asleep he hardly spoke to me. We had a pleasant day Sunday, going to church, where he was heartily greeted as a special guest, and out to lunch. I walked out to the car to tell him good-bye on that warm, sunny afternoon, and I remember thinking that it would be impossible to love him more. Our marriage seemed to have entered into a closer, deeper stage, and I marveled, wondering how it had happened.

The last thing we talked about before he left was the new sewing machine he had given me for my twenty-ninth birthday. Instead of being happy, as I should have been to have a machine that could do everything but talk, I had cried because he had traded in my beloved Featherweight. His comment had been that he would never understand women. But that afternoon, I told him how much I was enjoying the new machine and thanked him for giving it to me. After he drove away, I went inside and sat at that machine, trying to bring myself back together by beginning to put together pieces of a black maternity dress I had cut out that week.

On the next Sunday, he went to church twice, with two different sets of old friends. He wrote me about it that night, closing with "Take care of yourself and the bambino. All my love, Glenn." He mailed the letter on Monday and I got it Tuesday. On Wednesday, Tony and George came and told me he was missing.

6

A Brave Bird Singing

Well, my heart, we have been happy.
Let us snatch that from the wreck of things
But when the forest is choked with ashes,
While still the flame around its old nest flashes—
'Tis a brave bird sits on a charred limb—
And sings.[1]

I think I could count the times I have seen snow in my lifetime on the fingers of my two hands. The farthest north I have ever lived is Leland, Mississippi, and I would estimate its rate of snowfall (of

---

[1] Anonymous poem quoted in *The Desk Drawer Anthology: Poems for the American People,* compiled and selected by Alice Roosevelt Longworth and Theodore Roosevelt (New York: Doubleday & Co, 1937), p. 376.

the school-closing variety) at one or two times per decade. We have pictures of a winter wonderland scene when my sister Corinne was a baby, so there must have been snow in the mid-thirties. I remember making snow ice cream at school in first grade, which was a few years later. When I was in ninth grade, we had to go to school for several Saturdays to make up days missed because of ice and snow. And when I was a senior in high school, Old Man Winter shut things down again. I was corresponding with a young man whose National Guard unit, the Dixie Division, had been called up to serve during the Korean War, and I made daily treks through a mile or so of snow to the Stoneville Post Office looking for mail from Fort Jackson. These memorable meteorological phenomena usually occurred in the dead of winter—January or February. I don't recall ever experiencing snow for the holidays during my growing-up years. Every year, we dreamed of a white Christmas, along with Bing Crosby, while we witnessed only bleak, gray skies, brown ground, and stark, desolate trees.

It was different in 1963. On December 17, it started to snow. I remember, because that was the day a North American moving van made a delivery to me at my parents' home. In true Air Force style, friends at Davis-Monthan had closed my house in Tucson. I had requested that my bedroom furniture, Chantilly silverware, piano, and some personal items be sent to me, and the remainder of my household goods be placed in storage until I decided where I would live.

There was something unexpectedly comforting about unpacking those things, so fraught with memories of my life with Glenn—memories that bless and burn, as they are so aptly described in an old song called "The Rosary." I specifically remember coming across a photograph of Glenn that was taken in Australia upon his arrival there in the fall of the previous year. He was standing beside his airplane in his flight suit holding a beer, and his sleeves were rolled up, exposing his forearms—those strong, protective arms that I thought were capable of doing anything. How *could* he be gone? A new wave of incredulity swept over me. And the snow fell noiselessly outside, beginning to cover the landscape and cling to the tree branches. Standing there in that seemingly timeless and unreal cocoon, insulated from the busyness of the world, I faced afresh that *my* world had collapsed. The image of a forest fire, as portrayed in the poem quoted at the beginning of this chapter, perfectly expresses the way I perceived my circumstances. I felt as if I were "sitting on a charred limb" surveying the wreckage around me.

I was also trying to sing, like the bird in the poem. My song came from my little seed of faith that had been nurtured in the years and months leading up to this calamity. That faith had been fed from many sources, but none so forcefully as through Catherine Marshall's writing. As a result of reading (perhaps *digesting* is a more appropriate word) her book, *Beyond Our Selves*, I had come to believe that there was no circumstance that could not be turned to good by the God we served. It almost made the future seem like an adventure as I anticipated God taking control and directing me in the way He would have me go. By His grace, I knew enough to attempt to view my crisis from His perspective, and His working was immediately apparent in the inner landscape of my mind.

Only recently have I realized the extent to which He met my need in those early days of shock and adjustment. As I tried to make some sense out of my situation, one of the first impulses I felt was gratitude. That could have come only from the One who told us in His word to give thanks in everything. I was overwhelmingly grateful for my marriage to Glenn and what knowing him had meant to me. What a gift to have been married to a man who knew everything about me—all my quirks, weaknesses, and shortcomings—and still loved me unreservedly. Because of that relationship, I gained a genuine sense of self-worth I did not have before we met. When I saw how much value he, for whom I had so much respect, placed on me, I felt worthy to take my place in the human race. That was a permanent gift, still mine even though the giver was no longer present.

Then I was grateful for the ordering of circumstances in this most difficult transition. I was glad I had previously broken ties with the scene in Del Rio—my job, home, routine, and civilian associations. I had already grieved over losing those things and had recovered. If I had lost Glenn back when I was engaged in that phase of my life, it would have been much harder. I was also glad it didn't happen while we were in Alaska the previous summer, where I had no familiar support system. It seemed that the details of my life had been squared neatly away and I had been placed securely in the midst of my own people before the blow struck.

Another thing I was thankful for was that a few months earlier I had been led into the act of relinquishing Glenn into the care of God, for better or for worse, whatever that meant. In one of my more sane moments soon after it was confirmed that he had indeed entered the world on the other side, I said to myself, "Well, he was the Lord's anyway. If this is what He wants for him, it must be O. K." That knowledge was of unspeakable comfort. Why wasn't I blaming someone—the Air Force, the support team for the mission, the Cubans, Glenn himself? It would have been a natural reaction to seek some solace in placing responsibility for the fateful event on someone. I didn't do that because of the work of the blessed Holy Spirit. He simply would not let me "kick against the goads", but continually channeled His thoughts into my consciousness, like a life support system set up by paramedics in an emergency. I had divine first aid administered to me. "My thoughts are higher than your thoughts," we are told in scripture, and I was being fed those "higher thoughts."

At the outset of the crisis, I asked my sister, Corinne, to go to the library in Greenville to get Catherine Marshall's book, *To Live Again*. I remembered seeing it on a shelf in the library at Laughlin. I knew from the title that it was the story of Catherine's recovery from the grief that followed the death of her husband, Peter Marshall, but the time was not right for me to get into it when I first saw it. I didn't want to mourn while the bridegroom was with me. There would be time for that if he were ever taken from me, and I knew the book would help me do that. I didn't expect it, but that time *did* come, and this was it, so I sent for *To Live Again*. (Fortunately, my own copy arrived in the mail within a few days, a gift from Glenn's aunt, Jane Harris. The library would not have appreciated the hard wear I gave the book—numerous underlined and circled passages, with a tear stain or two here and there.) I really don't know how I would have gotten along during those days without it. I immediately identified with the author as she recounted the events surrounding the crisis of her husband's sudden departure from this life. In succeeding chapters, she opened her heart and candidly shared her fears and struggles as well as answers she found. As her story of being led to write the best-selling biography of her husband, *A Man Called Peter*, unfolded, hope was kindled in my spirit that I, too, could find a meaningful vocation in the years to come. *To Live Again* became my lifeline, like a life raft to a drowning man. Along with hundreds of others who read her books, I thought of Catherine Marshall as my personal friend. I wrote her a letter and the answer she sent back is still one of my treasured keepsakes. In the years since then, I have had occasion several times to participate in small group discussions where we were called upon to respond to a question that went something like "What person has exerted the strongest influence on your spiritual life?" My answer always is "Catherine Marshall". I knew her through her books in a way that would probably have been impossible in person without spending more time together than either of us had. When she died, I grieved as I would for any close friend, and I still find it difficult to believe that she is no longer on this earth.

Through her writing, she provided companionship for me during those dark winter days of 1963 and 1964. My grief was made even harder by the fact that in addition to losing my husband, I was separated from the support system of friends in the life I shared with him. Although people in Leland were caring and supportive beyond measure, they really didn't know me as did the people with whom I had lived the significant events of the past five years. I felt uprooted and cut off from most familiar relationships of the time. I longed to be understood. In the pages of *To Live Again* I met someone who, I felt, really knew where I was, and what's more, she pointed me in the direction of hope.

"You are not really trusting God until you are trusting Him for the ultimates of life,"[2] she wrote in a passage that is heavily underlined in my book. She went on to list the ultimates: Life and death, health,

---

[2] Catherine Marshall, *To Live Again* (New York: McGraw-Hill Book Company, Inc., 1957), p. 25.

economic necessities, the need to find one's place in the world, to love and be loved. Nearly every one of the "ultimates" she enumerated was a pressing concern for me at that time. I decided then that I *would* trust God with them.

Lest I sound super-spiritual in reporting this, I must say that it wasn't all that difficult to come to such a decision in view of my circumstances. It was God or nothing at that point. From my human view of things, there was no possibility of my establishing a meaningful, satisfying life again. I was simply unequal to the task, and I knew it. But thanks be to God, He doesn't require that our turning toward Him come with great sacrifice (although it may and often does) in order for Him to honor it. The path of my life since then shows that He took me firmly in hand. Further along in *To Live Again* I underlined these sentences:

> *Hand the grief, the failure, the disappointment, over to Me. I'm the only One who can take the broken things from life's trash heap, and by a divine alchemy make them better than they were before.*[3]

Somehow I believed they were true.

Besides giving me a basic orientation of trust, Catherine led me to the scriptures, which fed my growing seed of faith. Although I was fairly familiar with the Bible, I had very little experience in applying it to the specifics of my own life. I set out on a search for words from God that would reinforce the promise that He would rebuild my life. I marked the verses that spoke to me on the tissue-thin pages of my King James Version, dating many of them, and writing some on little cards for quick reference. I didn't know then that I was doing the wisest thing a child of God can do: go straight to His word for answers. I was simply trying to

---

[3] Ibid., p. 170.

survive. I was banking all my hope for the future on what one of His children, Catherine Marshall, told me was true, but I had to find out for myself if He really said it.

I was amazed to find that so many verses that only a short time ago had seemed archaic and remote to my situation suddenly sprang to life, as if they were written just for me. As things settled down to a somewhat wearisome routine after the tumultuous and busy days of December, I began to face the fact of my loneliness. One evening a frightening sense of apprehension came over me as I pondered the prospect of living without the kind of communication and understanding Glenn and I had. He had been my best friend. How, I thought, could I get along without being able to share my thoughts and feelings—the things that went on inside me—with someone who cared as only my husband had? I remember thinking that I felt as if I would explode if I had to keep everything bottled up inside. And then I read in the scriptures that there is One who does understand. There was ample evidence in the Psalms that He was "acquainted with all my ways." The very cries of my heart were recorded in the words of David: "Turn thee unto me, and have mercy upon me; for I am desolate and afflicted. The troubles of my heart are enlarged: O bring thou me out of my distresses." (Psalm 25:16-17.) In Psalm 69, he wrote "I sink in deep mire, where there is no standing: I am come into deep water, where the floods overflow me." Psalm 147 bolstered my conviction that my private pain was not really private when it told me in verse 5 that "His understanding is infinite."

Not only does He understand; He heals as well, according to verse 3 of that same Psalm: "He healeth the broken hearted and bindeth up their wounds." *Wound.* What an appropriate word. I pictured myself with an ugly, gaping wound, where something near my heart had been savagely ripped out. Could such an injury really be healed? I found other passages that assured me that God's very nature is to bring strength and wholeness to His children:

> ...weeping may endure for a night, but joy cometh in the morning...Thou hast turned for me my mourning into dancing: thou hast put off my sackcloth, and girded me with gladness; To the end that my glory may sing praise to thee, and not be silent. *Psalm 30:5c, 11-12a.*
>
> ...thou hast enlarged me when I was in distress. *Psalm 4:1b.*
>
> The Lord is nigh unto them that are of a broken heart; and saveth such as be of a contrite spirit. Many are the afflictions of the righteous: but the Lord delivereth him out of them all...The Lord redeemeth the souls of his servants: and none of them that trust in him shall be desolate. *Psalm 34:19, 22.*

What an encouragement that last phrase was to me: *No one who trusts in God will be desolate.* The word desolate described every scene that flashed into my mind when I allowed myself to contemplate the future. I could envision only loneliness and dreariness. But God was telling me right here in His word that I would *not* be desolate if I trusted in Him. That was something to hold on to! Other passages backed up that promise by proclaiming that God knows how to satisfy His children:

> O taste and see that the Lord is good; blessed is the man that trusteth in him. *Psalm 34:8.*
>
> O how great is thy goodness, which thou hast laid up for them that fear thee; which thou hast wrought for them that trust in thee before the sons of men! *Psalm 31:19.*

> The eyes of all look expectantly to Thee, for Thou art ever giving them their food at the proper time. Thou art ever opening Thy hand to satisfy the desire of every living creature...The Lord is near to all who call upon Him, to those who call upon Him sincerely. He fulfills the desire of those who revere Him. He hears their call for help and saves them. *Psalm 145:15-16, 18-19 (Berkeley version).*

The truths I was uncovering began to dominate my thinking, so that I usually maintained an optimistic outlook, but I was subject to frequent waves of doubt, which could send me to the depths of depression. I vividly remember one such occasion. One morning I was sitting on the edge of the bed putting on my stockings when the "father of lies", as Jesus names the devil in the book of John, hit me with a broadside: "Why are you so cheerful? Don't you know there's nothing to this God-business?" I was devastated. There I was, betting my whole life on God and His faithfulness. If He were not real, then I might as well give up. Life held no promise for me. That day, January 9, 1964, I wrote in my journal:

> *Do you or don't you believe that God has plans for us that are far better than our own? If you believe it, don't allow yourself to entertain doubts about it. Take each negative thought to God in prayer and let Him take care of it. So far you have had to accept that on faith. Now you will learn first hand that it is the truth.*

I followed the wisdom of that admonition a few days later, as evidenced in this entry for January 16:

> *Tempted to think God meant for me to spend the rest of my life in sadness and loneliness. This verse came to me: I had fainted unless I had believed to see the*

goodness of the Lord in the land of the living. *Psalm 27:13.*

Twenty-five years later, God would give me that same verse as the basis of the title of my life story, this book, *To See His Goodness.* It sums up my pilgrimage, because I couldn't have made it had I not believed in His goodness. The key at that sad juncture years ago, as well as at every stage along the way, was to fortify myself with the Word of God. Another verse gave me encouragement at the time:

> Remember ye not the former things, neither consider the things of old. Behold, I will do a new thing; now it shall spring forth; shall ye not know it? I will even make a way in the wilderness and rivers in the desert. Isaiah 43:18-19.

What was my present situation but a wilderness and a desert? God's promise of a *way* and *rivers* were sweet words indeed.

That keeping the faith was a continual struggle can be seen from a journal entry on January 28:

> *In case I should forget, let it be recorded that this experience is indeed the hardest thing I ever had to endure—a constant fight to keep the dark cloud of despair from descending. The only answer is to cling to the promises of God and trust in "firm, dry faith" that He will keep them. I long to "taste and see that the Lord is good." I believe it now, I have experienced it in the past, and I expect to be shown the truth of that verse in full measure in the future.*

I found that the enemy is endlessly resourceful in coming up with ways to get at me. When I had managed to counter his lies by finding proof in God's word that my future was safe in His hands, I began to doubt my ability to follow His plan. "O. K.," the devil seemed to say, "so He does have good things planned for you. The problem is that you're so inept that you won't be able to do your part. You'll mess everything up." Some of my most cherished portions of scripture helped me answer those taunts:

> Trust in the Lord with all thine heart; and lean not unto thine own understanding. In all thy ways acknowledge him, and he shall direct thy paths. *Proverbs 3:5-6.*

> And though the Lord give you the bread of adversity, and the water of affliction, yet shall not thy teachers be removed into a corner any more, but thine eyes shall see thy teachers: and thine ears shall hear a word behind thee, saying, This is the way, walk ye in it, when ye turn to the right hand, and when ye turn to the left. *Isaiah 30:20-21.*

> Delight thyself in the Lord; and he shall give thee the desires of thine heart. Commit thy way unto the Lord; trust also in him; and he shall bring it to pass. *Psalm 37:4-5.*

> Thou wilt shew me the path of life: in thy presence is fullness of joy; at thy right hand are pleasures for evermore. *Psalm 16:11.*

In one verse, a little preposition, the word *for*, jumped out at me and brought a wonderful truth to light: *I will cry unto God most high; unto God that performeth all things for me.* (Psalm 57:2). I underlined and circled that unlikely little three-letter word. It couldn't be more clear. God would do it *for* me. It didn't matter that I was unable to rebuild the structure of my life. *He* was able!

I live in a city today that has five radio stations and one television station devoted solely to Christian programming, so good, solid Bible teaching is almost always available at the turn of a dial. It takes some effort for me to recall how it was twenty-five years ago, when Christian broadcasting was in its infancy and cassette tapes were a thing of the future. I was essentially limited to the printed page for spiritual input. But I received some unexpected and timely encouragement when our church had a series of meetings they called a revival in February. The evangelist was a young minister from another church in the North Mississippi Methodist Conference. The minute he opened his mouth, I knew he was personally acquainted with the Lord of whom he spoke. I specifically remember his account of having come from a place of worrying about his wife, Nancy, to whom he was obviously devoted, to one of trusting God with her. I surely identified with that, having engaged in a similar struggle myself. I've forgotten the content of his sermons, but I do remember feeling as if I were walking on air as I left each service. I knew our God was real. I thought to myself at the time that this young preacher (he was about my age—we were both young) would not remain for long in the small town church ministry. With his living faith and unusual ability to communicate it, I knew he would be led to larger audiences, probably in a large city church. I thought of him from time to time in the years that followed, wondering what had become of him. His name soon escaped my memory, but I never forgot hearing him.

Sixteen years later, in 1980, I attended a seminar at Oral Roberts University. On the second night, the Dean of the School of Theology there, Dr. Jimmy Buskirk, was on the program. When he was introduced, it was mentioned that he was from Mississippi, so as he began to speak, I settled in to enjoy a talk by someone who spoke the English language like I did. I was enthralled in his account of being healed of a debilitating eye disease when he happened to refer to his wife, Nancy. I felt the way those disciples Jesus joined on the road to Emmaus must have felt when they suddenly recognized Him when He broke the bread. I had the same sudden recognition of one of the Lord's servants. Here was that preacher who had been like an angel of light to me back when my world was so dark. I later heard that he became senior minister at a large church in the midwest; the prediction I made when I first heard him came true.

The lowest point for me during those dark days in 1964 came one bright, crisp February morning when I went to the closet to get a dress to wear. As I stood trying to decide which of the bedraggled maternity frocks hanging there I should put on, a dark heaviness seemed to press down on me, and with a deep sigh, I said, "Why couldn't I just die?" The answer came immediately as my thoughts turned to the little life inside me, and I knew I had a reason to live.

My journal for the month of February contains increasingly frequent references to the baby. At the top of a list of "heart's desires", which is what I called my prayer list, written that month is "a strong, healthy, happy baby." As the time drew nearer for him to be born, he began to take on a personality for me. I always thought of him as a boy, although in those days there was no way to know the sex of a child before he arrived. My memories of that last month of pregnancy include a picture of me propped up in bed on my reading pillow talking to the baby. I used to tell him what good friends we were going to be and what fun we would have together. It wasn't known back then that it is a good thing to talk to unborn children. I just did it because I felt like it.

When March 4, my due-date, arrived, I sat around all day, suitcase at hand, waiting for the signal that it was time to go. What a letdown it was when the day passed and everything was the same. I endured several such days before the time finally came for me to make the trip to the hospital in Greenwood, where, on a stormy Saturday afternoon, my precious son was delivered by Caesarean section. (So much for falling off a log.) Presiding over his birth was Dr. John Lucas, who ushered into the world a major portion of the Mississippi Delta population (including me) during his long practice. I first knew the baby was here when a nurse waked me up in what sounded like a very loud voice and said, "Mrs. Hyde, you have a little boy." I asked, "Is he all right?", and after being assured that he was, promptly went back to sleep.

When I was finally wheeled out of the recovery room, in a somewhat more wakeful state, the hall was lined with my loyal, supportive family: my parents; my aunt, Bessie Bell; and my cousins, Bill and Bettyann Weilenman. Our togetherness at that moment is solidified for me in Bill's greeting to me as they rolled me by. He said, "Mary, you done excellent!" He was referring to a family anecdote about my uncle, Dick Gerdes, who, like my father, was a cotton ginning specialist. While on a visit to his hometown in south Texas from his post at a major state university, he appeared on an early morning radio farm program. Afterward, he went into the local cafe, where he was greeted by one of the farmers gathered there, who said, "I heard you on the radio this morning, Dick; you done excellent." That unsuspecting farmer gave us a good phrase to use whenever we wanted to give someone a strong compliment. When Bill told me that day that I "done excellent", he was saying much more than mere congratulations. He was saying, "We have a common history, you belong to us, and we're in this together." In that moment, I knew what "family" meant. It is one of my warmest memories.

Later, a nurse brought my big boy to me and told me he weighed ten pounds and two ounces. He was *beautiful,* even with his little pointed head that so many hours of trying to be born had given him. He had a head full of long, dark hair, and over his eyes were little "puffs" like the ones I had loved on his father. His name was never discussed. Everyone just knew he would be Joe Glenn Hyde III.

The family contingent was exhausted after standing by for a day and a half waiting for our blessed event. My mother immediately came down with the flu and spent the next week in the Leland hospital. Since I was about forty miles from home, I had very little company during my ten days in the hospital, but I got a lot of mail and managed to run up a sizable telephone bill talking to friends in Tucson and to the Hydes in Georgia. Many people celebrated with me, which was a great source of comfort. I am reminded on a regular basis of how enthusiastically little Glenn was welcomed into the world when I polish the shelf full of silver cups given to him. We were blessed to be the recipients of so much caring.

After about five days, a nurse came in and cheerfully asked how I would like to keep the baby with me in my room. The idea of being responsible for such a helpless little creature terrified me. I thought for a minute, then told her I wasn't ready for that. (If this happened today, I would have already been home with him by then. Ours must seem like a pampered generation to young mothers now.) Later that day, they brought him in and set up his cardboard-box bed next to mine. I hadn't understood that the nurse wasn't asking me if I wanted to keep him; she was telling me. It seemed he was the only baby in the nursery and they were going to give it a good cleaning before it filled up again. My full-time motherhood began sooner than expected, but it was a definite blessing. Although it came later than what is recommended today, that was our bonding time. I held him, nursed him, and talked to him when he was awake, and gazed at him in wonderment when he slept.

And I cried tears of joy mixed with tears of sorrow—joy that this little person had come to live with me, and sorrow that the one I longed to share him with was not there. One particularly poignant scene sticks in my mind. One afternoon when I was bathing him and admiring his little body, I thought of how big Glenn had enjoyed his nephews, Jeff and Jerry Hyde, when they were babies. He and Richard, the twins' father, were like two big boys, just delighted with those babies, commenting on their physiques, and noting how "solid" they were. To know how proud he would be of his own son and that he would not have the opportunity to enjoy him pierced my heart. This was the first of many such realizations, because I would instinctively see my child at each stage of life through his father's eyes.

A few days before I went to the hospital, my mother-in-law had sent me a poem (which unfortunately I have lost) that likened raising a child to an archer placing an arrow in his bow, pointing it in the right direction, and letting go. It was undoubtedly based on the passage in Psalm 127 that says *As are arrows in the hand of a mightyman; so are children of the youth.* I must have had that in mind when I wrote in my journal on our last day in the hospital:

> *Little Glenn...is truly beyond my expectations in every way... May I be a flexible, yielding bow in the hands of the Master as we send this little arrow toward its mark. Remember that God always has the best prepared for His children.*

On my thirty-first birthday, we went home, and I entered a new chapter of my life. Sadness, while not entirely absent, would be overridden by joy. I still had some grieving to do, but the dark cloud was gone and the sun was shining again.

7

The Fool Hath Said

On a hot August afternoon, a North American moving van pulled away from a pleasant little white house shaded by tall walnut trees on Manila Drive on the north side of Jackson, Mississippi, having just deposited all my worldly goods. I moved there a few months after my baby was born. "Here I am," I thought, as the van turned the corner at the end of the street, "stuck. The Air Force is finished with me now. I'll never move again." I felt as if I had been left on the sidelines, forever cut off from the real world, envisioning a pleasant but somewhat flavorless life stretching out in front of me. What followed were two surprisingly good years in Jackson. This capital city of the Magnolia State had been a favorite spot of mine since high school days when we used to attend Beta Club conventions at the Heidelberg Hotel and socialize on the steps of the old capitol at night (expressing our grownup-ness by smoking Kool cigarettes). When my sister Rachel took a teaching job there after graduating from Millsaps College that spring, we decided to live together. Later, I planned to enter Millsaps and take courses to qualify for a teaching certificate.

Every place to which I have moved has had its own set of "angels" to help me get established. In Jackson, they were LaNelle and Tom Nash. LaNelle had been my roommate and close friend when we taught in Shaw and Dallas. They gave tirelessly of their time, energy, and friendship to help me feel as if I belonged in the community

Establishing my own home was comforting, and I had fun arranging familiar things in a new place. We converted one bedroom into a den, Rachel and I each had a room, and a little room on the front of the house was a perfect nursery. Running a household gave me deep satisfaction. I studied cook books, even checking some out from the library, to plan meals, never shopped without a list, saved trading stamps, and watched for weekly specials. I don't think I had taken housekeeping so seriously since those first weeks in Del Rio.

At the Galloway Methodist Church I became active in the choir, and I joined the Jackson Choral Society. The people I met were kind and friendly. When the second semester rolled around, I registered for two elementary education courses at Millsaps. School was something I had always known how to "do", so this, too, was fulfilling.

After a year, Rachel married Ray Lewand and they moved to Texas, where he entered the Graduate School at Baylor University. In the fall, I took a full load of courses at Millsaps, in addition to teaching a small number of piano students. A lovely young woman who loved Glenn came every day to keep things running at home. I was grateful for my routine after spending so many months in limbo. I remember thanking the Lord for all this one morning as I sat in the Kroger parking lot waiting for the store to open. Lula Mae was at home with Glenn, and I was getting ready to shop and then head to Millsaps for a nine o'clock class.

I knew, however, that this comfortable life-structure would have to change soon. I was nearly finished with the required education courses and needed to make a decision about what to do next. The logical move would be to get a teaching job, but that prospect didn't appeal to me at that point. I wanted to do something that would allow a flexible, more relaxed schedule while Glenn was little, and that would put me in a position to meet more adults than I thought would be possible in an elementary school setting. It just seemed there was no such occupation that matched my training and ability, which caused me no small amount of anxiety when I thought of the future.

The answer began to come one Sunday morning at church while I was sitting in the choir. Out of the blue, a most appealing thought dropped into my mind: "Why don't you go to graduate school?" One of the courses I was currently taking and enjoying was Elementary Music Methods, taught by Louise Byler, who had taught music in Leland when I was in school. The idea of working on a master's in music education was something I could get excited about. I began working on that idea, trying to figure out how to do it. There was no school in the Jackson area that offered such a degree, so I would have to move.

A short time after the possibility of going to graduate school occurred to me, my good friend from Air Force days, Helen Doering, called one night to tell me that Jim Sala, husband of our friend Mary Nell had lost his life in Viet Nam. I immediately called Mary Nell at her parents' home in San Antonio. When we talked about what she might do, she said she thought she would move to Austin and finish her business degree at the University of Texas. All the bells rang for me right then. I didn't know how I would pull it off, but the University of Texas was the school for me too.

Mary Nell and I met in Austin the following August, two weeks to the day after Charles Whitman went up on the observation deck of the Texas Tower with a cache of firearms and opened fire on everything in sight. As I walked across the mall in front of the Main Building, the horror of those moments seemed to hang over the campus like a pall. I was never able to look at the flag poles there without remembering news reports showing people crouched behind their bases trying to keep from being gunned down. I walked past those flag poles to the Music Building, where I was able to see the Music Department Chairman, Dr. Bryce Jordan, and found that a place had been prepared for me there. There just happened to be an opening for a teaching assistant in music education and I was hired for the job.

Mary Nell bought a duplex high on a hill on appropriately named Alta Vista Street in south Austin that very week. She became my landlady and we lived there together when I moved to Austin..

I returned to Jackson and divided my belongings—some went to the Hydes in Georgia, some to my parents' attic, some to the Nash's garage, and the remainder was moved to Austin. Two busy weeks later, Glenn, who was two and a half by then, our wire-haired terrier, Dubby, and I headed west in my white Oldsmobile. I was going back to Texas, the state I loved, to go to graduate school, which had been a secret but only recently recognized desire of mine. Life was getting exciting again.

Again there were angels on hand to help me get established. They were two couples I had known at Laughlin. Eva Hardeman, with whom I had worked in the choir at the base chapel, and her husband, Pat, had settled in Austin upon his retirement. It was with them that I stayed during my August visit there. Pat is a gentle, kind man, and little Glenn was especially drawn to him. When we were at their house, he wasn't happy unless he was sitting in Pat's lap or helping him do some work. Pat was of immeasurable help to me, installing curtain rods and other things that could have been big problems. Once he drove all the way from his house in far north Austin to Alta Vista Street to straighten an overhead garage door track I had bent by driving into it.

The other friends to welcome us were the Leatherwoods. Art had flown in the squadron with Glenn, and I had become acquainted with him and his wife, Maxine, at the base chapel. They had been the first family to move from Del Rio to Tucson when the wing was transferred, and Glenn and I had visited them in their home there on our way to Alaska. I couldn't have known then what a significant part they would play in my life for years to come and what good friends we would become. Art had retired from the Air Force a year before we went to Austin and was completing a degree at the University. We had corresponded before I moved there, and he had given me information about the school and encouraged me to come. They took us in like their very own. They were so kind to keep Glenn for me when I needed help that

I'm afraid I took advantage of them. My son and I both have fond memories of those days.

Our living situation in the duplex proved to be ideal. Mary Nell and her daughter, Pamela, whom I had first seen moments after she was born six years earlier in Del Rio, lived in one side and Glenn and I occupied the other. There was a double garage between us. We had the best of both worlds. We each maintained our privacy, but we could run back and forth at all hours without going outside. It was especially good to be able to visit at night after the children had gone to bed. I never felt as if I were alone.

One of my less admirable traits is that the more I think I have things under control, the less I depend on God. Things were shaping up so much to my liking that I spent less and less time communicating with Him or even thinking about Him. The last time I remember praying a specific prayer was just before I took the Graduate Record Exam. My undergraduate grades were high enough for the University of Texas Graduate School to accept me conditionally, but I would have to make an acceptable score on the GRE to remain. I was worried about this, because it had been a long time since I had done anything with math besides balancing a checkbook, and I didn't do so well at that. That prayer was answered when I made the required score with eighty points to spare. At that point, I said, in effect, "Thank you, Lord; I can take it from here."

I didn't give up church; I just let my *personal* relationship with the Lord dry up. I joined a large Methodist church near the University, where I was a regular, dependable choir member. We sang the great music of the church, which was especially edifying for me. The churches had not recognized a need at that time for ministry to singles, and it was very difficult for me to find a place there, apart from the choir. I thought it was important for Glenn to grow up going to Sunday school, so we always went. The only adult class available besides one for couples was one for ladies, most of the members of which were at least my mother's age. I attended that one and met some lovely ladies, but generally felt like a misfit.

In my work, I had no problem fitting in. It was my good fortune to work for Miss Charlotte DuBois near the end of her long, successful career as a teacher of teachers. Being her assistant was enriching and challenging. She loved music and people—including children—and directed her efforts toward bringing the two together. I learned from her about children's natural attraction to the best in music and in her teaching she modeled ways to make it meaningful to them. Two years later when I had completed my Master of Music degree I knew how to do something—teach music.

The time was not right, however, for me to go into full time teaching, as I felt I still needed a flexible schedule to accommodate my mothering role. Going to school gave me so much satisfaction that I decided to stay and work toward an advanced degree in education. I bought a little house on a cul-de-sac off beautiful Shoal Creek Drive on the north side of town, sent for the furniture I had left in Mississippi, and put my roots down deeper in Austin. My living situation seemed most satisfactory—a home of my own at last and what I thought was a meaningful occupation, working toward another academic goal. I didn't know I was headed for one of the most barren periods in my life.

Looking back on that time, I can see little signs in my thought life that showed a growing dissatisfaction with the way things were going. I remember sitting in my car in the driveway one morning thinking how naive I had been to think God would put my life together again. My idea had been that he would send along a husband who would love me and be a father to Glenn. I was not so aware of my own need for a man in my life as I was of Glenn's need. All his life, I had made sure he knew he had a dad of his own. Trying not to idealize him or set him up as some kind of impossible example he would be pressured to emulate, I talked of his dad often, repeating little anecdotes that would make him seem like a real person. I still think that was a good thing, but it didn't meet his need for a real flesh-and-blood dad. Among my "blessing and burning" memories were ones about big Glenn's rapport with children. The little boys in our neighborhood in Del Rio used to come to our kitchen door and ask, "Can your daddy come out and play?" I have home movies of one of those mornings. Glenn had devised a way to keep the boys out of his way while he mowed the lawn. He attached a rope to the lawnmower and told them they were to pull the mower while he actually pushed it. They dutifully went along ahead of him and he directed them like a drill sergeant when it was time to turn. (Describing it now, I wonder if it was all that safe, but it did turn out all right.)

Thinking of these things, I knew Glenn was missing a vital part of his life. I was relieved recently to hear psychologist Dr. Kevin Leman say on the "Focus on the Family" radio program that a single mother shouldn't try to be both mother and father. He eased my conscience to no end when he said a mother didn't need to go out and play ball with her son. Being inexcusably out of touch with sports, I somehow overlooked the possibility of my own involvement there, but I knew my child needed to be doing sports and masculine activities with someone. These thoughts led me to remark that morning in the driveway on my naivete in believing before he was born that God would meet all the needs left by his father's absence. It struck me then that there was no way any man was going to love and accept Glenn as his own son, and I knew that would be necessary before I could marry again.

I now know that it was God's grace that had prevented, and would continue to prevent for a while longer, my remarriage. In my rebellious spiritual posture I would surely have made a disastrous choice. The truth of the matter was that even if Mr. Wonderful had come along then, I would not have recognized him, because I was still emotionally married to my child's father. I wasn't the least bit interested in dating. In my sixth year of widowhood, it hadn't even occurred to me to take off my wedding ring. I was going to have to face the fact that my husband was never coming back, let go of the past, and look toward the future. Consciously, I had done that, but sub-consciously I was still clinging to my marriage, as evidenced in the dreams I had about Glenn periodically. In each of them, he came back to see me, but I knew it was just a temporary visit. I would wake up in the middle of begging him to stay, "because this little boy needs you." One Sunday afternoon, when he had been gone for about the same length of time that we were married, a little over six years, I had a dream that ended all that. As in the other dreams, he came to see me and I begged him to stay. To my surprise, he told me he didn't want to stay. I could think of just one reason why he wouldn't want to stay with me, so I asked him if he had found someone else. When He said he had, I replied, "She must *really* be something!" He answered, "She is." When I waked up, I knew my marriage was over. I was emotionally free.

I'm no expert on dreams, so I will not attempt to interpret that strange one, except to say that I certainly don't think it had any basis in fact—there was no "other woman." I believe it simply represented the only way my mind could process the fact that he really was not coming back—ever, and that he wouldn't want to if he could. It was a little like being pushed out of the nest. I was really on my own.

At about the same time, my thinking on spiritual matters took an ominous turn. I never deliberately turned my back on God, but I made the mistake of trying to interpret Him in light of all my new-found knowledge. When I discovered the humanistic psychologists, I thought I had found the link between secular and religious thought. Hadn't Jesus said that He came to give us life, and that more abundantly? The psychologists seemed to refer to the same thing when they spoke of the self-actualized life.

Regrettably, I didn't think the comparison through far enough to see the profound differences or to question the premise from which the psychologists operated. They said that people were basically good, and that they lived self-fulfilled lives to the degree that their needs were met. These self-fulfilled individuals would presumably be kind, loving, generous, patient, tolerant, peace-loving people. I liked that. It was so much more uplifting than that old-fashioned doctrine that said we are all born sinners in need of a Savior. The fact that one can hardly pursue a self-actualizing life, requiring as it does the satisfying of one's own needs first and foremost, without being self-centered didn't bother me. I had learned a peculiar and convenient device of our time—to select from the holy scripture those passages that reinforce one's position, writing off the rest as irrelevant or somehow flawed. Thus I didn't consider all the teaching Jesus gave us about denying ourselves. Such familiar passages as the following never entered into my judgment:

If any man will come after me, let him deny himself and take up his cross, and follow me. For whosoever will save his life shall lose it: and whosoever will lose his life for my sake shall find it.[1]

Verily, verily, I say unto you, Except a corn of wheat fall into the ground and die, it abideth alone; but if it die, it bringeth forth much fruit. He that loveth his life shall lose it; and he that hateth his life in this world shall keep it unto life eternal.[2]

Those verses tell us how to attain the fully-functioning, self-actualized life—by dying to self. I missed it because I paid attention only to that part of the input I was receiving that came from the humanistic side.

Even so, I had a need to reconcile my very real and meaningful experiences with a personal God in the past with my new intellectual understanding. One night, standing in front of the mirror putting on make-up, I put it all together. I thought I had come had come

---

[1] Matthew 16:24-25
[2] John 12:24-25

up with an original idea, but it's really as old as the hills. I decided that there was no objective God out there; He was simply a creation of our minds that served to personify the truths of living. The "truths" (all this business about self-actualizing) were real, not God. He was a figment of each person's imagination. And upon reaching that conclusion, I became a first-class fool: *The fool hath said in his heart, There is no God.*[3]

The devil had told me years before that I was so stupid I would mess up God's plan. He was right about the first part—I *was* stupid. But God was too gracious to let me get so far off course as to foil His plan. He let this poor, dumb sheep go wandering off into the wilderness, but He never let me out of His sight. He would bring me back, but I would have to become thoroughly miserable before coming to my senses.

---

[3] Psalm 53:1.

8

Back From the Far Country

Every Saturday night in the city where I live, a Christian radio station broadcasts a sermon by a famous preacher, Dr. Donald Gray Barnhouse, now gone on to glory, whose sermons swept thousands into the kingdom of God. I recently heard one of those sermons, which was as relevant for me as it must have been for its original audience a half century or so ago when it was first preached. He spoke on the passage in the fifteenth chapter of John, where Jesus says, "I am the vine, ye are the branches; He that abideth in me and I in him, the same bringeth forth much fruit; for without me ye can do nothing." He pointed out that a Christian can choose to abide or not. If he chooses not to abide, he is still a Christian; his work just doesn't amount to anything. That work is described in the third chapter of First Corinthians, which says that Christ is the foundation, but we can build on it with gold, silver, precious stones, wood, hay, or straw. Then he gave an illustration of a plant, one of whose branches was constricted by a wire. The branch began to wither, but when the wire was removed, it regained its health and bloomed within a short time. He likened the wire to the constraints of sin. (Dr. Barnhouse preached in a time—or at least in a place—in which sin was considered an acceptable subject to bring up.)

It is not a practice of mine to take notes on sermons I hear, especially on the radio (though it is surely a good one), but I wrote the main points of this one in my journal because it seemed to explain what had happened to me during the time after I relegated belief in God to the realm of superstition. It was as if a wire were cutting me off from the Source of life, and everything began to dry up. The first thing that happened was that I became depressed. I would wake up in the morning surrounded by a black cloud. None of the activities and projects I had been able to lose myself in mattered anymore. The degree I was working toward and the career that presumably lay beyond it were of no interest. I didn't *want* a career. Doing school work became an uphill struggle. I described my condition at the time by saying I had run out of steam. Suddenly I was tired of academia, but I could see no place to go from there.

Then I started to date. I found it most awkward at first. It was like being sixteen again and starting to go out for the first time. I didn't know whether to open the door for myself or wait for my date to let me out of the car. I couldn't decide what to order from a menu. And finding an excuse to go the ladies' room was a major challenge. Just as I had at sixteen, I learned how to function in that setting, but it seemed so ridiculous to have to cover that ground again.

I met some nice men, but the one I flipped over was the wrong one. Fortunately, he failed to flip over me, but that didn't keep me from devoting two years of my life to the frustrating and emotion-consuming undertaking of trying to convince him that we were made for each other. This new relationship soon took its place at the center of my life, soaking up most of my time and energy. With the small amount of each that was left, I plugged along at school, finishing my course work and passing the qualifying examination for a doctorate. All that remained was writing a dissertation.

That I was able to get so much done is amazing, because I was always upset. It seemed that everything was out of control. During that distressing time, the high point of my week was choir practice on Thursday night. I would go there nervous and tense and come home relaxed and peaceful. I think it was because of the holiness of the material we dealt with. Virtually everything we sang was based on scripture. Even though I took it all with a grain of salt, spending an hour and a half singing God's word was healing, because the Word is alive. I specifically recall the tenderness I felt singing "He Watching Over Israel" when we did *Elijah*. A lost sheep was hearing from afar the Shepherd, whose voice she knew.

Wild horses couldn't have kept me from choir practice. It was God's tranquilizer. At one point, I asked my doctor if he could give me something to calm my nerves because I was going through a hard time. He said I needed to take care of the thing that was upsetting me instead of dealing with the symptoms with medication. Wise man, that doctor. He probably saved me untold grief. (There are undoubtedly situations in which medication is advisable and even necessary, but this was not one of them.)

Adding to my stress, decision time was looming on the horizon again. I had managed to find part-time employment at the University for each of the five years I had been there, but I didn't have the nerve to apply for another graduate assistantship. Besides, I needed to start earning a real salary. Glenn would be going into second grade, and the time seemed right to try to get a teaching job.

I was supervising student teachers at the time, and they were tuned in to the teaching job market. From them I learned the names of several school districts around Houston. I knew nothing first-hand about Houston, but it was booming then and seemed like a promising place to establish the next phase of my life. I was rapidly reaching the limit of my toleration of the insecure relationship I had gotten myself into, and the only possible relief I saw was to move. (I don't know why I didn't consider terminating the relationship; that would have been a lot simpler.) I made several applications and spent two days in Houston interviewing. Within a couple of weeks, a big white envelope containing a contract from the Spring Branch School District arrived in the mail. It wasn't the ideal job for me, as I really wanted to teach music. Spring Branch did not have music specialists in their elementary schools then, but I had heard such glowing reports about the district that I signed the contract to teach second grade and sent it back by return mail.

If I thought a change of scenery would help my emotional state, I was wrong. After a gigantic effort of packing, moving, and getting my house in Austin ready to rent, Glenn and I found ourselves cramped into a two-bedroom apartment on Houston's west side. Apartment dwelling in the city was not nearly as glamorous and "cool" as I thought it would be. In fact, nothing was glamorous or cool. I was uniquely unsuited for my job. Nothing about it matched my interests or way of doing things. I just couldn't get with the program and dreaded going to work every morning.

As my custom was, I went downtown and found my way into the choir at the First Methodist Church, a stately old structure at the corner of Main and Clay. At the end of my first choir practice there, an attractive woman in the soprano section sought me out and introduced herself. Her name was Janet Kivett, and she was secretary to the minister of the church, Dr. Charles Allen. She made me feel welcome and appreciated in the choir and indicated that she would like to be my friend. Driving home that night on the Katy Freeway, my heart glowed at the thought of having a new friend. I have wondered since if she knew how badly I needed one.

The following Sunday, Janet suggested that I come into town that night and meet her for the evening service. How unusual, I thought, to have church on Sunday night. I hadn't heard of that since I left Leland. I accepted her invitation and really liked the service. The preacher was an associate minister named Mouzon Biggs, who talked about God as if He were real, not some abstract idea. At the end of the service, the lights were lowered and people were invited to go to the altar to pray before leaving. I'll never forget how warm and protected I felt as I knelt there. It was like coming home. I didn't pray; how do you pray to a figment of your imagination? But I remember thinking, "Wouldn't it be nice if this were all true?" And then the most outrageous idea I could imagine came to my mind—the idea of breaking off that debilitating relationship I had struggled for so long to make work. It wasn't a command, or even a suggestion. It was just an idea, like "Have you ever thought of this?" (I hadn't.) As I knelt before God in His holiness, He gently but unmistakably put His finger on the thing that had become god in my life. I didn't know all this was going on then, but, like a lost sheep, I heard again the distant call of the Shepherd's familiar voice.

The fall months dragged slowly and miserably by. Everything I did required tremendous effort. I would come home from school and collapse on the sofa, too tired to lift a finger. Nothing was working. I hit bottom on a cold January afternoon. Houston had experienced an uncommon winter storm that left the wrought-iron steps up to our second-story apartment covered with a thick layer of crystal-clear ice. Where Glenn and I were going on such a day I can't imagine, but as we started gingerly down the stairs, I slipped and landed on my bottom several steps down. My whole world seemed to tumble in with me. I could take no more. Nothing in my life was working. I just sat there, unable to move, and sobbed. Glenn stood patting my back and probably wondering what in the world was wrong with his mom.

Shortly thereafter—maybe it was the same night—I knelt beside my bed and prayed, "Lord, I don't know if you are there or not; I haven't thought you were. But if you are, I want to live my life your way—even if I have to spend the rest of it alone." No bells rang, no sense of peace—or remorse. I crawled into bed that night not knowing if my prayer had gone beyond the ceiling. But events began to take place that left no doubt that God had assumed direct control of my life again. All He was waiting for was an invitation, no matter how weak and tentative the faith that accompanied it.

On a Sunday afternoon a few days later, I realized that I was emotionally free. The hook that had held me in an unsatisfying but somehow irresistible relationship was gone. It was as much a miracle as any dramatic physical healing. "Who needs this?" I asked myself, and I broke off the relationship that I had thought I couldn't live without.

I had come to that place again where I had to let go of my solutions in ordering my life so God could do the job right. An adventure lay ahead that I could never have imagined.

9

Equally Yoked

One night in February, my new friend, Janet, stepped into my car in front of her southwest Houston apartment, and we drove to one of a pair of apartment towers nearby to attend a "seminar on psychology," as she described it when she asked me to go. It was to be conducted by a friend of Mouzon Biggs, the pastor whose preaching had done so much to draw me back to the truth. This friend had visited Mouzon in the church offices that day and had invited Janet to the seminar series he was leading every Tuesday night. She thought these might be of interest to the two of us, so we went.

Greeting us in the club room on the first floor was an attractive man in his mid-forties with silver-gray hair and horn-rimmed glassed whom Janet introduced to me as Bob Brown. He was comfortable and charming in his role as speaker and group leader. Before an audience of about ten people, using several visual aids and with much colorful personal application, he gave a presentation of material that he said came from two books by a Catholic priest named John Powell: *Why Am I Afraid to Love?*[1] and *Why Am I Afraid to Tell You Who I Am?*[2] The point that I got from his talk that night was that our relationships could thrive only on emotional honesty. After his talk, he skillfully led a discussion period. That night I saw a gifted communicator talk about a subject that was obviously near and dear to his heart. My conclusion, after going through my usual routine of sizing up single men, was that he was nice, but not my type. (The subject matter under consideration obviously was not my primary concern.)

He must have arrived at a different conclusion about me, however, because he called the next day and asked me out that weekend. We spent a lovely Saturday evening having dinner at one of Houston's outstanding restaurants and attending the Alley Theater, where we saw Thornton Wilder's *Our Town* (which reminded me of Leland and comes to mind every time I visit the cemetery there).

Bob was very verbal and did not hesitate to talk about himself, which, as it turned out, was an interesting subject. I learned that he grew up in the state of Iowa as the son of a Methodist minister. He served in the Army near the end of World War II, graduated from a church-related college in his home state, married, and took a job as a teacher. He later went to work in the oil industry, moving up fast, and arriving in Texas in the early sixties to direct the marketing division of a Houston-based company. While

---

[1] John Powell, S. J., Why Am I Afraid To Love? (Allen, Texas: Tabor Publishing, 1967).

[2] John Powell, S. J., Why Am I Afraid To Tell You Who I Am ? (Allen, Texas, Tabor Publishing, 1969).

he was advancing up the corporate ladder, however, a more sinister and subtle course was underway in his personal life. Long before he knew it, Bob had started down the slippery slide of alcohol addiction. Things began to fall apart several years before I met him, when, after nineteen years and four children, his marriage broke up on the reefs of the insidious disease that often destroys its victims before they know they are being attacked. Next to go was his job. Undaunted, he went on to form his own investment business, which flourished for a while, and married again.

This period of seeming well-being was marred by an underlying restlessness and foreboding. Once he was providing financial counseling for a woman from another city in his office, and he was suddenly captivated by her face. The peace and radiance reflected there reminded him of the women he had known in his father's churches when he was a child. He told her this and asked her what it was that gave her such a look. Her answer was, "Everything I have I owe to God, and I found Him through Alcoholics Anonymous." Bob never forgot that exchange. Within a few months, he found his way to an AA meeting in west Houston. After viewing a film that detailed the progress of the disease of alcoholism, he knew that was his problem. He said it was a great relief to find out he was sick, not crazy. He never took a drink from that night in the fall of 1968 until the end of his life.

Acknowledging his addiction and going into the AA twelve step program marked a turning point in his life, but it did not signal an end to his problems. In fact, the worst was yet to come. In the months that followed, his second marriage failed and his business took a downward turn.

Equally Yoked

While outwardly his life seemed to fall apart, inwardly the Lord was clearly at work. One morning when he was in his second year of sobriety, sitting at his desk, he suddenly broke into uncontrollable weeping. Knowing that he needed help, he thought of a couple he had met in AA who he knew went to church, and made a desperate call to them. When the wife heard his voice, she recognized the severity of his condition and told him to stay right where he was while she sent someone to help. Then she called the First Methodist Church and asked for the senior minister, Dr. Allen. He was not in, but Mouzon Biggs, an associate minister, responded. No one on the staff was better qualified to meet Bob where he was than Mouzon, who understood alcoholism from experience in his own family. He dropped whatever he was working on and went over to Bob's office immediately. The outcome of that encounter was that the two of them became close friends and Bob went back to church after a very long absence. He told about going first to the Sunday evening service and sitting on the back pew, hidden in the dark under the balcony. As the weeks went by and his self-image improved, he gradually moved closer to the front, eventually singing in the evening choir. By the time I met him, he was attending Sunday morning services, presumably an indication of further progress. When Bob told his story, he said he met God in AA, but he found Christ in the church. Mouzon was most generous with his time, and Bob visited him often to talk. When the rewards are passed out on the other side, Mouzon is going to get a big one for picking Bob Brown up and helping him to walk again. Bob would need the spiritual strength he was gaining, because another blow lay just around the corner.

One night on a rare evening at home in the rented room he described as the closest he came to "the bridge", the proverbial domain that represents "the bottom" to an alcoholic, he became ill. He sensed that a heart attack was in progress and called a doctor whom he had met in AA. The doctor arranged for an ambulance to pick him up and met him at the hospital, and Bob survived his first heart attack. He later heard that his doctor friend had had a "slip" (that is, he had started drinking) that week and the night Bob called was his only night home. He was convinced the Lord had a hand in his receiving the help he needed.

He had been reading Merlin Carothers' book, *Prison to Praise*, and had been trying to put its message into practice by praising God in everything and trusting that He was able to bring good out of any circumstance. When he regained consciousness in the hospital after his heart attack, his first thought was "How could anything good come out of this?" Immediately the thought came, "Well, you've always wanted to stop smoking." Something deep in his spirit answered "Yeah!" He never had a desire to smoke from that moment. A decades-long chain-smoking habit was supernaturally broken.

His problems were far from ended, however. A second heart attack led to by-pass surgery and complete inability for months to make a living. When I met him, he was just getting on his feet physically after surgery and was attempting to reestablish himself in the business world. He told of the hard days of convalescing, sometimes not knowing where his next meal would come from. He ate a lot of tomato soup when Weingarten's grocery put it on special for ten cents a can. A friend from AA came by his place faithfully once a week with food. Another AA associate let him use a car that had belonged to a deceased parent. It must have been humbling for Bob, so conscious of his image, to drive around in a far from new "little old lady" car. (When I met him, he was driving a new Oldsmobile convertible, much more in character.)

He recounted all this to show how the Lord had taken care of him. He never missed a meal and always had transportation, a necessity in a city like Houston. As he put it, the Lord had to "knock me down so far there was no place to look but up." (I think what he meant was that the Lord had allowed all his supports to fall away, not that He knocked him down, but I got his point.) And looking up he was. It was obvious to me that he was a yielded vessel to the Lord. I understood that, but I wasn't ready to accept the premise unconditionally. When he suggested that I start praising the Lord instead of complaining about my unsatisfying working situation (a la Merlin Carothers), I answered that I had tried all that and it didn't work. He must have thought he was out with a real pagan.

That evening together was the beginning of a solid friendship. I continued to attend the Tuesday night seminars, usually going for coffee with him afterward, we went out on weekends—and talked—and talked, and we attended the Sunday evening service at our church together. One Sunday night when we were in the choir and Mouzon was preaching, one of those thoughts that carries an unmistakable mark of significance dropped into my mind: "You've always wanted to serve the Lord through your marriage." It was true. Deep in my heart was a desire to do the Lord's work as a team with my husband. The prophecy of the

Class of '51 in my high school yearbook had predicted that I would "direct a seminary". The story behind that was that I was dating two pre-ministerial students at the time. Then when I was married, I used to fantasize about Glenn and me working full-time, living on faith, with a Christian organization of some kind (an idea he would have been unable to comprehend had I voiced it—he was already doing what he was supposed to do). I knew that God had some special work cut out for Bob, and in that moment I felt I was being called to stand with him in it. I argued with the Lord a little, not because I didn't want to obey, but because I felt I didn't deserve it. I had been so unfaithful to Him that I thought I should do some penance by staying single for a while. The impression I got was that He was more interested in my getting on with His work.

One of the ministries of the church we attended was regularly scheduled seminars to take a psychological test and study the personality profile it yielded. It had helped Bob so much that soon after we started dating he insisted that I take it. On all traits except two, we were different, but we were alike when it came to getting along with other people. According to the results, we were both "frank, direct, and straightforward." The validity of the instrument, at least on that point, is borne out in the fact that we didn't waste time playing games that night after my surprising revelation. When we left church, I told him of the thoughts that had come to me during the service. He must have agreed, because our relationship was never the same. No longer were we "just friends". I remember thinking as we cruised down the freeway, "How did this happen?" Why was I sitting in the middle of the front seat instead of respectably on my side as I was when we drove into town? A page had been turned.

To say that I "fell in love" with Bob then is probably not accurate. It was more a case of being able to see into his heart—his goal of reestablishing his life in the face of what appeared to be insurmountable difficulties and his true desire to serve God. I understood and empathized to the point that I wanted to identify with him in all he faced. I don't know that I loved him at that point, but I was surely committed to him, which may be closer to real love than our usual interpretations of the word.

We made no public announcement of our commitment to each other. He wanted to be in a position to support a wife before entering into a marriage. Because of a deep-seated but as yet unrecognized fear of financial insecurity, I wholeheartedly agreed. Complicating the situation was the fact that he had a discouraging amount of debt from so many months of inability to work. Nevertheless, we believed the Lord would work it all out, and proceeded to live one day at a time.

He directed his energy toward establishing himself in the investment business, but his heart was in more spiritual pursuits. Nearly every night was taken up with meetings along that line. Monday was AA night; Tuesday his group met to discuss Powell's books; Thursday he attended a "witness group" at St. Stephens Episcopal Church; and every Friday I joined him for a praise service at the Church of the Redeemer. Sunday, of course, was devoted to our own church. The education director there, Mrs. Mildred Parker, heard from Janet about the discussion group he had been leading and thought this would be a good class to add to the Sunday school program. Bob was delighted when she asked him to start such a class. As he put it, he had been "sick and tired of being sick and tired" long enough. The possibility of teaching a bona fide church school class offered a chance to do something positive.

The new class was advertised in the church paper for several weeks prior to its first meeting as, for want of a better name (after all, it *was* about psychology), the Human Potential Class. A sizable group of people gathered on the appointed day. Bob was obviously exercising his gifts as he brought the group together and focused on his lesson of relationships—with God, others, and ourselves. The response was enthusiastic.

One of the first orders of business was to choose a name for the class. Bob didn't like the temporary name of Human Potential. I heard him teach many times on John 15: *Apart from me you can do nothing.* He knew all too well his poor potential without the Lord, and objected to the name because it gave a false idea of what the class was all about. The title he put forth was "Christians Under Construction." When the vote was taken, however, the old name won and the class has been called Human Potential to this day.

Bob had experienced failure and disappointment on so many fronts and shared about it so freely that the class began to attract people who didn't have everything all together (as Christians are "supposed" to). He soon saw a need for people to respond to the ideas presented on Sunday and to share with each other in small groups, so he started a Wednesday night sharing group. In addition, he had many calls for individual counseling. His ministry became all-consuming. While this area of his life was flourishing, the wage-earning side hardly got off the ground. The verse he operated on was "Seek ye first the Kingdom of God and all these things will be added unto you." He trusted that his needs would be met as he continued to do the Lord's work.

Then another crushing blow struck. One night near mid-April, he was at my apartment working on my income tax return when he had some of the old familiar chest pains he thought he would never have again after surgery. I went with him several days later to his cardiologist to get the results of the tests that had been immediately ordered. There he found out that one of the by-pass grafts had collapsed, but no new surgery was recommended because his heart was in no condition to withstand it. I'll never forget my feeling of complete despair as we drove away from the Medical Center along tree-lined Sunset Boulevard. Here I was, "peering over the edge of eternity" again. He said he felt as if he had been turned out onto the street to die.

The following Friday night, instead of going to the service at the Church of the Redeemer, we went to the Mariott and talked. When we finished, many of our preconceived notions had been set aside. We agreed that we were in this together, that we were supposed to get married, and that the only thing holding us back was the lack of a guaranteed income for Bob. Then I decided to commit everything I had to the Lord and trust Him to provide for me. It would be possible for us to swing it financially if we could look on the resources I brought into the marriage as the Lord's and not as mine. This also required trusting Him with the future, because the little nest egg I had tucked away for my old age would not last forever. We faced all that, talked it through, and decided to get married early in June.

When we left the restaurant, I felt as light-hearted as I can ever remember. This was fun.

No marriage counselor would have advised us to make the decision we made. We broke all the rules. The situation was full of ingredients for disaster. Right or wrong, we no doubt were able to act so decisively because of the other trait we shared on our test results: "You normally make decisions quickly. Your ability to react quickly in most situations enables you to get at the essential facts." Reviewing our action years later convinces me that the "essential facts" we saw then were the right ones to act on, no matter how foolish it might have appeared on the surface.

On June 2, 1972, before a surprisingly large gathering of family and friends, I walked down the aisle of the church that had brought us together to festive organ music played by my friend from U. T. Graduate School days, Russell Schulz. Rev. Mouzon Biggs conducted the Service of Holy Matrimony before the beautifully carved altar, and we became man and wife.

That I was aware of the extent to which I was laying my economic security on the line is clear to me when I remember my thoughts as we exchanged our vows. I was thinking that I would no longer receive a survivor's check from the Veteran's Administration each month and that Bob was ineligible for life insurance. It was a tremendous step of faith. But then, isn't any marriage?

10

Precious In the Sight Of the Lord

Laity Lodge is a retreat center in the Texas Hill Country located on the H. E. Butt Foundation Camp grounds near the small town of Leakey. I would be hard-pressed to count the times I've been there, but the first time was with Bob on the day we celebrated our eighth day of marriage. In the many Christian circles in Houston in which Bob moved, he had heard several times about this place, so when we drove in the vicinity of Leakey on our return from a wedding trip to the Davis Mountains in West Texas, we decided to drop by and see it. That's a joke, because you don't just "drop by" Laity Lodge. We went to considerable effort to find out where it was. Upon reaching the turn-off from the highway, it was necessary for me to disembark from the car and open the gate while Bob drove through. Continuing for some distance on a descending gravel road, we suddenly found ourselves poised at the edge of a river, where a reassuring sign said "Yes, you drive..." So drive we did, right down the bed of the Frio River, which fortunately was shallow at that point. Shortly after following the road out of the water, the Lodge appeared before us. Howard Butt describes the place this way in his book, *The Velvet Covered Brick*, which was written at about this time:

> You find Laity Lodge in the country of 1100 springs—"Frio" means Cold River—hidden in the vastness of the Texas Edwards Plateau mountains. Up high, looking down on the fish, the boats, and the swimmers below, its great hall juts out—cantilevered above the lake. For twelve years this place, dedicated to God, has spoken as an innovative center about renewal—for persons, families, and churches; for clergy and laymen of all kinds, sorts, sizes and descriptions; for all denominations.[1]

We "happened by" this hidden paradise on Saturday afternoon of a weekend retreat in progress. The participants were enjoying free time for study and recreation, and the seminarian assistant on the staff was able to show us around and tell us about the program. Bob was impressed to see one of his spiritual mentors (by way of her book and recorded testimony), Gert Behanna, in deep conversation with one of the retreat participants when we walked through the Great

---

[1] Howard Butt, *The Velvet Covered Brick* (New York: Harper & Row, 1973), p. 38.

Hall. We learned that an upcoming weekend retreat had several openings.

Back in Houston the next morning at the Human Potential Class, Bob invited all who were interested to go with us to Laity Lodge later that month. Ten members of the class drove over for a retreat led by its director, Bill Cody, and Roger Fredrikson, then pastor of Sioux Falls' First Baptist Church. Bob and I were awed by the spiritual insights we gained by participating in such a functioning segment of the Body of Christ. The weekend was of great personal significance for him. With much emotion, he shared at the final wrap-up session about what it had meant to him to relate to fellow Christians on the level that had been possible there.

At home again, we began our life together as a family a few weeks later when Glenn returned from his annual summer visit in Mississippi with his grandparents. Converting from single-parent status to a full-fledged family was not easy for any of us, but it was one of the most profound benefits of my decision to marry Bob. Glenn was eight years old and desperately needed a strong male model and authority figure. To this day I appreciate Bob's dedication to his fatherhood duties. His own children were grown and he surely had thought he was finished with childrearing, but he didn't hesitate to give priority to Glenn's direction. He was fully prepared to assume his role as spiritual head of the family.

Soon after we got engaged, we had our first family meeting and Bob read from Ephesians 5 and 6 about how each member of the family is to function. He laid out the ground rules up front. As he came in as a strong new leader and imposed structure on a situation best described as "hang-loose", we all experienced stress. Many times I thought he was too hard on Glenn, and he, of course, thought I was entirely too lenient. Glenn loved Bob and took great pride in referring to him as "my dad". He undoubtedly benefited in ways I will never know. In the years since, when I have been tempted to worry about him, I have been encouraged by reminding myself that God provided a father for him at a critical stage in his development, even when I was not aware of how much he needed one. (Regretfully, in spite of the encouragement, I still succumb to worrying.)

At the beginning of our marriage, we made a budget (rather, Bob made it; I don't know how to do that—still) and figured out how much income we would need. The figure we came up with, in addition to my teaching salary, was an amount well below what Bob had earned in the past, so we felt confident that we would be able to make ends meet. But it was uncanny how everything he went into that promised to generate income flopped. The fact was that his heart was turned to ministering to people, and he was unable to go after business with enough drive to provide adequate income.

Each month, we withdrew enough from savings to fill the gap. As much as I claimed to trust the Lord—and I did try—each withdrawal put a knot in my stomach. Bob and I had communication problems in other areas, but this was a place where we were completely open with each other. He knew how nervous I could become on the subject and was most patient and understanding, even though my anxiety undoubtedly added to his stress. Catherine Marshall wrote about financial security as one of the "ultimates of life" and pointed out that to trust God with those is what real faith is. I still needed to learn how to do that.

I can say without hesitation that Bob's life was poured out for other people, which is remarkable in light of the fact that by his own admission most of his life had previously been lived with a definite orientation toward himself. He seemed to be driven to minister to others. Sunday morning was his platform, where he taught a growing number of class members. After each lesson, people would tell him how he had spoken directly to a situation they were facing of which he had no prior knowledge. A dramatic example of this was the morning he walked up to a man named Stan sitting on the front row and said, "Take Stan here..." and proceeded to place him into a hypothetical scenario to illustrate his point. Stan was overcome. Everything Bob had said was actually the case. He and his wife went home with us for lunch that day and we became the best of friends. They would later take their places among the "angels" who have helped me over points of transition.

The sharing group on Wednesday night continued to grow. The group met in a large parlor-like room on the fifth floor of the education building. Bob began with a short devotional talk. Then the group would divide into smaller groups to share in relation to the input received in the large group. The cardinal rule, which was strictly enforced, was that no advice would be given. Seeing in later years how quickly the trust in a group can evaporate as a result of a self-appointed expert attempting to solve people's problems has convinced me of the wisdom of that ground rule. We ended with a social time over coffee and refreshments.

We never knew where some of those people who showed up on Wednesday night came from. Many of them had no connection with the church. They had just heard of the group and came. Bob was adamant about the meeting taking place every week as scheduled. During the summer, the church sponsored a barbeque each Wednesday at its west side facility out on Bellaire Boulevard. It was suggested that we move the sharing group there for the convenience of those who wanted to attend the barbeque beforehand, but he insisted that it meet in its regular place downtown. He didn't want anyone to come seeking help and find no one there.

Not surprisingly, several alcoholics surfaced among the people who heard Bob openly share his experience, so he started an AA group that met each Tuesday night. That group, like the others, thrived.

When we moved into a larger apartment near the end of Memorial Drive, one of the first things we did was to pray that our home would be a place where people could come and find spiritual direction and support. That prayer was answered repeatedly. I never knew who I would find there when I came home from work. Once I walked in to find a young widow who had come to the class several Sundays before. By the time she left that night, the tears that her red eyes betrayed were gone and she was laughing—with us and at herself. She became a good friend.

Early one evening, we answered a knock on the door to find a distraught friend nearly at the point of collapsing from the pain of rejection. She had just found out her husband had moved in with another woman. Bob was wonderful with her and probably helped to save her life.

Then there were countless people with drinking problems who met with Bob in his study to inventory their lives. He told me amazing stories at the end of the day of people he had happened to encounter at critical times whom he felt he was able to help. I witnessed his ability to say exactly the right word to a hurting soul in just a brief exchange many times. People told me later how a single sentence from him had encouraged them or clarified an issue. He had remarkable insight into people's needs. His life was bearing much fruit.

All in all, what we had in those days was a church within a church, functioning as a true Christian community. The Human Potential class became a family. A few years ago I was invited back to speak there about its founding and its founder. It would have been easy to idealize Bob and depict him as the super saint he probably appears in the previous paragraphs, but I felt that I should portray him as he was, warts and all, of which he had no shortage. Acknowledging him as a weak, fallible human being shows all the more the work of the Spirit in his life. When I was organizing my thoughts for the presentation, it came to me that Bob's life perfectly exemplified the way we are all called to live. The virtues extolled over and over in the Scriptures are trust and obedience. Nowhere does it say that we must do everything right and make no mistakes. Bob fell short of perfection often. Sometimes he took things into his own hands and made a colossal mess, but he was quick to repent and partake of the Lord's grace. When he flew off the handle and let someone have it, he repented and asked their forgiveness—and probably the Lord's as well. Once I heard him call and apologize to a bill collector with whom he had just lost his temper and hung up the phone. Doing the right thing was important to him, even when it was humiliating.

He used to say there were two times when he had trouble trusting the Lord. One was when things were going good and the other was when they were going bad. He was speaking of the human condition. Trusting doesn't come naturally, and good times as well as bad have their hindrances to faith. But Bob did trust.

I can testify that he was far from the perfect husband. Living with him was most trying at times. (I hasten to acknowledge that he could—and most likely would—make a similar statement about me.) He was demanding to the point that I often felt I failed to measure up to what he expected of me. This was especially true in the area of communication.

From studying John Powell's book, *Why Am I Afraid to Tell You Who I Am?* he was convinced that a marriage could thrive—perhaps even survive—only when the level of communication that Powell calls "gut-level" is in operation.[2] (To begin with, that description is somewhat offensive to my "southern belle" sensibilities.) This involved reporting of feelings, even if this might upset the other person. I just reread that book to refresh my memory on Bob's orientation, and I have no doubt that the author writes the truth. But putting it in the hands of someone as zealous as Bob can be dangerous. He came on so strong with his advocacy of deep sharing that I dug in my heels and resisted. It seemed to me that the negative feelings he reported were usually brought on by some thoughtless

---

[2] see John Powell, S. J. *Why Am I Afraid to Tell You Who I Am?* (Allen, Texas: Tabor Publishing, 1969) pp. 57ff.

act of mine, and I invariably reacted defensively. Whenever he said he needed to talk, I thought to myself, "Uh-oh, I wonder what I've done this time." Ideally, I should have remained emotionally neutral and helped him work through whatever it was in him that caused him to react negatively to my actions. I never reached that level of maturity.

Then he became impatient with me when I did not cooperate by sharing my feelings. He was convinced that I was suppressing all kinds of negative emotions that would erupt one day and blow us apart. He may have been right, but the truth was that by the time we got around to our sharing time at the end of the day, I was usually too weary to know what I thought, much less what I felt. On a typical day, I would have arisen and gotten Glenn and myself off to school before Bob's feet ever hit the floor, had taught all day, gone shopping, prepared supper, and accompanied him to some meeting—and loved doing it, but I was in no condition for any deep sharing. We could have used a third party to help us over this impasse, and no doubt we would have gotten to that had we had more time.

From the perspective of years, I understand Bob better and can see that his intensity in this area actually derived from his fear of failing in another marriage. He knew how dangerous it was for things to build up between a couple and was almost fanatical about taking measures to ensure that such a thing not happen to us. I'm grateful for that and regret that I didn't have that insight at the time, although I'm not sure what I would have done with it. I once heard someone say on the radio that there is such a thing as beating a marriage to death with too much honesty, and I understand how that could happen. Our communications needed a healthy dose of compassion to temper some of that honesty. The subject of emotional honesty was a sore spot all through our time together, but our ship of matrimony managed to sail on triumphantly "under the mercy," to use a wonderful phrase I learned from reading Sheldon Vanauken's books.[3]

Another stress during those days was Bob's health, although being so conscious of the Lord's hand on his life usually made it easier for me to trust in that regard. I never accepted the sobering assessment he had been given about his heart condition as the last word. When Kathryn Kuhlman came to Houston for a series of meetings, we were there every night, singing in the choir We heard the moving testimony of a policeman who had been healed of cancer at one of her meetings and we witnessed what appeared to be authentic healings during the week. I started to readjust my thinking and went home to read the Book of Acts with new eyes. This was when we began to think that God might reach down and heal Bob.

Later, I found a book by a Canadian doctor describing his success in treating heart patients with massive doses of vitamin E. Bob called his clinic in Ontario and got specific instructions for this treatment. We counted calories, weighed food, and followed strict nutritional guidelines. Bob read Dr. Cooper's book, *The New Aerobics* and cautiously embarked on a running program. I read the companion aerobics book for women and started running myself. (Needless to say, I was

---

[3] Sheldon Vanauken. *A Severe Mercy* (New York: Harper & Row, 1977) and *Under the Mercy* (Nashville: Thomas Nelson Publishers, 1985).

carried away.) One night a young couple in the Human Potential Class came to our apartment and said they felt led to lay hands on Bob and pray for his healing, which they did. We believed he was getting well.

That summer, Bob received a small inheritance from his father's estate. He used most of it to pay some personal debts, then put the remainder in traveler's checks, and we set out on a three-week trip that would take us to London, Ontario, to the clinic with which he had been conferring. We dropped Glenn off in southwest Missouri for the very first session of Camp Soaring Hawk, a camp run by my cousins, Jane and Heno Head. (Glenn holds the distinction of being the first camper to sign up at Soaring Hawk, thanks to his grandfather, who enrolled him shortly after the Heads bought the camp the year before.) Driving through Iowa, we stopped to visit some of Bob's friends from years past, had lunch with a couple who had been friends of his parents, and dropped in on an elderly aunt.

In Canada, we spent a day at the clinic and received a most encouraging report. They confirmed our opinion that he was steadily improving and that he should continue in his present lifestyle. The news was liberating, and he seemed to shed his invalid mentality. Worrying about his health was one concern he could set aside.

We had a wonderful trip back, driving through the stunningly beautiful Finger Lakes district of New York, then visiting Hyde Park, the birthplace of the man who presided over our childhoods. After a brief but delightful tour of New England, we stopped for several days in Washington. We had spent each evening of our trip watching rebroadcasts of the Watergate hearings and felt we were really participating in history when we passed Senator Lowell Weiker, whom we had watched on the tube, in the hall of the Capitol. From Washington we drove through the Shenandoah Valley and to Hickory, North Carolina, to visit one of Bob's cousins. It was a carefree, pleasant time.

Heading west on Interstate 40, we came to Black Mountain, where I had spent three summers during high school attending Camps Montreat and Merri-Mac. At Merri-Mac we learned that Macky no longer owned the camp, but she still lived in her house next door. I was afraid she wouldn't remember me after so many years, but I underestimated her. She immediately knew who I was and even inquired about my sister Corinne, who had attended camp with me. I told her of things I remembered fondly about camp, especially her sitting on the porch at Camp Montreat singing "Read Your Bible" to us every morning. She laughed sheepishly and said, "That was 'cause I wanted y'all to read your Bibles." I never saw her again. A dozen years later, I would return for a camp reunion and memorial service for her. (Thank you, Macky; I'm still trying to read my Bible early in the morning.)

We continued west to Missouri, picked Glenn up at camp, and drove on to Houston, arriving home on a Saturday night in time for Bob to shut himself up in his study to prepare his Sunday school lesson.

Soon after we returned, Bob was reconciled with the only one of his children from whom he had been still estranged since the unfortunate breaking-up of his family. One Saturday night, all four of his children—Bob III, Linda, Susan, and Bryan—came over to our house for dinner. There was much laughing and joking and it was evident that those young people adored their father. I sensed that a lot of healing had taken place to make such an evening possible.

After church the next morning, we loaded the car again and left for the Texas Hill Country. Bob and I checked in at Laity Lodge for a week-long study retreat, and Glenn was enrolled in one of the youth camps on the grounds. We had chosen this particular week because Roger Fredrikson, who had led the first retreat we attended there, was on the leadership team. Bob felt a kinship of spirit with Roger, and although their acquaintance had been brief, regarded him as kind of a mentor. Joining Roger on the team were Louis Evans, minister of the National Presbyterian Church in Washington, and Myron Madden, a clinical psychologist from New Orleans.

Louis taught each morning from the Book of John. This was the most instructive Bible study either of us had been exposed to and we were fascinated. Bob's appetite was whetted for more. We stayed up late Wednesday night talking about the possibility of his attending seminary. He knew that he was called into ministry, and he wanted to be formally trained for it. This excited us both. We didn't know how we would swing it, but I had been through this kind of thing before. I knew there would be a way if it were meant to be. The next day he made an appointment with Roger for Friday afternoon to discuss the idea.

By Thursday, after four days of studying, sharing, feasting, praying, playing, and laughing together, the retreat participants had become a close community. The events of that day would bring us even closer together.

That morning during the break, Bob motioned to me to come out to the water fountain. Glenn was there getting a drink after a tennis class at the courts nearby, and we had a brief family reunion. That afternoon during free time, Bob visited those same courts for a game of tennis while I stayed in the room and read some material for my dissertation, a project I planned to resurrect for the rest of the summer.

Later we dressed for dinner and went to the dining room for the usual feast. After the meal, as we stood around the balcony overlooking the lake, I heard Bob make a most significant statement when someone asked him what he did. Instead of describing his work with the sound of success and stability, as he usually did (doesn't everyone?), he said, "I do whatever the Lord tells me to." That may have sounded like a cocky answer, but it was true. He waked up every morning asking what the Lord wanted him to do, and the answer often had nothing to do with going to work. I thought his handling of that question indicated that he had finally accepted the fact that his status as a person derived not from professional achievement but from obedience to his Lord. No longer was it necessary to put together an acceptable-sounding description of his work. This seemed to me to represent a major point of arrival in his spiritual life, but I don't know that he realized it.

When we convened for the evening session, the chairs were arranged at the end of the hall, where huge windows gave a magnificent view of the steep side of the canyon across the lake. The evening commenced on a note of joy and playfulness as we sang "Lord of the Dance" and danced the "Bunnyhop" around the room. As I sank comfortably into the soft cushions of a gold sofa, winded from all that jumping around, Roger began his talk. He started to tell what we in Texas call an "Aggie" joke, except that his story concerned some other abused group instead of Texas A & M students. Before he reached the punchline, Bob turned a strained, ashen face to me and said, "Honey, I don't feel well. Would you go and get my medicine." I rushed over to our room, grabbed the bottle of pills, and returned to the hall to find him lying with his head in Louis' lap and people encircling the sofa. Suddenly he went into a kind of seizure and asked us to say the twenty-third Psalm. As everyone there recited this familiar passage with its comforting lines, "Yea, though I walk through the valley of the shadow of death, I will fear no evil, for thou art with me", Robby Robinson, a high school principal from Hollywood, who had become Bob's close friend during the week, came forward and began to administer mouth-to-mouth resuscitation. Time stood still as Robby steadily continued to pour out his strength for his friend. I couldn't say how long it was. I remember standing in the middle of the floor wrapped in Roger's arms and thanking God that He was in control. (I had finally learned the lesson Bob tried to teach me on our first date, to thank God in everything.) I was sitting with Ruth Fredrikson on a sofa opposite the one on which Bob lay when a doctor finally arrived, examined Bob, and came across to talk to me. He was kind enough to include a medical explanation for what had happened to him, but the only part I understood was that my husband was gone.

I walked over and looked at him lying where we so recently had sat together and said in a voice that sounded as if it came from some place other than from me, "Good-bye." I was thinking, "Well, good-bye—if you say so." I knew everything was fine with him when I saw the complete lack of stress on his face. I pictured him being welcomed on the other side by a multitude of saints and thought how amazed he must be to be there. He had run the race and had won the crown, but I, who had poured so much of myself into his race, felt abandoned. I knew he was all right, but what was to become of me? Then I was aware of the assemblage of saints on this side of the Great Divide who had just seen him off and were holding me up at that moment. The God who had promised never to leave or forsake me was with me in this time of high crisis in a most tangible way through His Body.

Before Bob's body was taken away, he was covered with a sheet and we sat around his deathbed for an impromptu worship service. It couldn't have been more meaningful if hours of planning had gone into it, because of course the Spirit directed. Louis opened by reciting in his deep, resonant voice "Let not your heart be troubled; you believe in God, believe also in me..." It wasn't somber; there was joy and thanksgiving—and awe. When we dispersed for the evening, we all knew we had been in the presence of God.

Years later I found the verse in Psalm 116 that says "Precious in the sight of the Lord is the death of His saints," and I thought that it must have been written for Bob. His passage from this world to the next was indeed precious. Why else would it have been orchestrated with such care to every detail? I know the Lord loves us all, but he must have a very special place in His heart for Bob, who tried so hard to serve Him. I think He honored that commitment by throwing that awesome party the night he went home.

Roger asked me later what Bob had wanted to discuss with him. When I told him of his interest in further study, he said, "Now he has gone to the greatest seminary there is." I think that's true. And knowing Bob, I would guess that by now he has managed to gather around himself a little group of saints to teach them everything he knows.

The small group I participated in for the week was led by Myron Madden. On the morning of the day Bob died, we had discussed handling grief, and I had shared about how much it had hurt when my first husband died, but that every time I allowed myself to feel the pain, it hurt a little less. Finally, the pain was defused; I could remember things and it didn't hurt. Myron had affirmed me and I had been glad to find out I had done something right. He was one of the first people to speak to me after the doctor told me Bob was gone. I don't remember his exact words, but the essence was "You'll be all right, Marianne; you know how to do this." My answer, which came back like a reflex, was "Yes, but I didn't want to do it again." Here I was facing the same question I had faced ten years before: Would there be another life for me? And I was scared. I didn't want to leave the warmth, support, and protection I felt that night and venture into the great unknown out in the world. I thought our church family in Houston cared only about Bob—not for me. I was wrong.

11

Many Members, One Body

Certain days in the course of a lifetime, for one reason or another, stand out in bold relief, with details indelibly imprinted on one's mind. The day Bob died is one of those days for me, as is the day following. On the night of the dramatic turn of events at Laity Lodge, I was able to sleep, largely thanks to a lovely lady named Penny Ruhman, who graciously volunteered to spend the night with me. We talked for a long time and then she sent me off to sleep with a good back rub. Our room overlooked the lake and the first sight to greet me the next morning was the path on the other side where just twenty-four hours earlier Bob and I had gone for an early morning run. A wave of sorrow mixed with incredulity swept over me at the fresh realization that he was gone. It was almost inconceivable that I couldn't tell him all about the night just past. He would have been so interested and at no loss for words to offer his commentary and opinion. (He *would* have had an opinion—and numerous comments.) My mind soon turned, however, to the more practical tasks ahead. I had to get Glenn and break the news to him, and somehow we had to get back to Houston. As it turned out, I had lots of help with all of that.

Before breakfast, Roger, Louis, and I boarded a station wagon and drove over to the youth camp. Glenn must have wondered what was going on when he was brought to me and these two strangers and we solemnly sat down together. Roger was so gentle as he told him of his dad's death. In straightforward, factual, and very caring terms, he described the scene exactly as it had happened. When the four of us returned to Laity Lodge, Myron took Glenn aside to talk while I ate breakfast. As part of His abundant provision for us during this crisis, the Lord even provided a counselor for that little nine-year-old boy to help him sort out his feelings about Bob's death.

I'll always remember that breakfast, because that was when I met Keith Miller. He had come in during the night and was eating, as I was, at an odd time. I know writers are just plain people, but I have enough country in me to be impressed by someone who has had a book published. By then Keith had published several books, so I was *really* impressed. When Bill Cody introduced us, I said the dumbest thing. He had spoken at my sorority alumnae group at the Kappa house in Austin when I lived there and I had been unable to attend, so upon meeting him, I blurted out how sorry I had been to miss his talk. This led to some teasing of him for being a provider of sorority programs, and I felt I had managed to come across as an "air head" instead of an intelligent, informed reader of his books. It did, however, provide some levity for the occasion, which, as the Bible says, "doeth good like a medicine."[1]

Before the morning meeting convened, we left for Houston in the care of Melvin Gray, a fellow Mississippian who had come to Texas to attend seminary. He drove us home in Bob's red convertible and later caught a ride back to Laity Lodge with some Houstonians going to the next week's retreat. I was completely comfortable with Melvin—maybe it was our common Mississippi roots—and felt free to voice all my concerns, which were many, as we made the nearly day-long trip.

High on my list of worries was finances. Bob had kept up with all that, mainly because doing it stressed me out, not because I couldn't do it. I wasn't a helpless widow; I just didn't know how much cash we had on hand or how much a funeral would cost. I should have remembered how thoroughly the Lord had taken care of every detail of this ordeal so far and known that he surely had that part of it in hand as well. As it turned out, His provision amazed me. In the previous spring, Bob had heard from two separate insurance companies that premiums had been paid on policies on his life from built-up cash value, and that if he wanted to keep them in force, he should send in the back payments. He had no recollection of those policies. He had let them go, he thought, when everything fell apart during his illness. We sent in the premiums, and I remember him calling into the kitchen from his study one night while I was cooking supper and saying, "Honey, I'm putting these policies in the bottom desk drawer in case you need them." That was a kind of message I didn't like to hear, so I only half paid attention to it.

---

[1] Proverbs 17:22.

But now it was suddenly very important. The first thing I did when we got home was to make a bee-line for the desk and found that the policies were indeed there. The upshot of all this is that when I added up what we had used of savings during our thirteen months of marriage, it matched to the dollar the amount of life insurance proceeds I received after the funeral expenses were paid.

But riding in the car between Laity Lodge and Houston, I didn't know that. I was also concerned about going through everything that awaited me in Houston alone. After all, I was a step-mother to Bob's children. They might not want to have anything to do with me. The Sunday school class adored Bob, but I didn't know if their affection extended to me. Melvin listened to me talk about all this and was a rock of support. I would have been surprised if someone had told me then that I would one day be an Episcopalian and would belong to the church family where he was rector. That has happened.

When we drove into the carport behind my apartment that Friday afternoon, I knew I wasn't alone when Jean Fraser and John Etzold came running out to the car. Jean and I had become good friends by talking on the phone every Tuesday night when our husbands were at AA, and John was a dentist who came to the sharing group but belonged to another church. The house was full of people from the Human Potential Class. All of Bob's children were there, and they couldn't have been kinder to me. I was right back in the middle of the same kind of loving fellowship I had left at Laity Lodge. God's people, I found, are a wonderful network.

I soon realized what a sense of personal loss people felt over Bob's death and wanted to include them in it, so I volunteered to teach the class on Sunday morning and tell them about his homegoing. The room where we met comfortably accommodates about forty people, but it was packed beyond capacity that day, with people even sitting on the floor. I told the story very much as I've told it here, and we grieved and celebrated Bob's life at the same time. When I finished, Jim Robinson, the class president, stood up and announced, "I think we just heard our new teacher." I was as surprised as anyone there to hear such a thing. It had never occurred to me that anything I would say in the role of teacher would be of interest to anyone, but when Jim said it, I knew he was right. My life for the next two years would center around that assignment.

The first morning I was home, I got up determined to continue the fitness program I had engaged in with Bob. I put on my running clothes and went out to run the mile that we had measured off around the apartment complex, but I simply did not have the stamina to make it. Why was that? I hadn't been sick; and surely missing one day of exercise was not enough to leave me in such bad physical shape. Through that experience I learned first-hand the interrelatedness of our physical and emotional states. I had experienced a tremendous emotional shock and it had affected my whole being. It would take some care and time to recover. Fortunately, my friends understood this and I didn't have to go through the process alone. For several days, someone was on hand just to be with me day and night. On about the tenth day, I felt strong again—ready to exercise as well as to enjoy some privacy.

One afternoon I was lying down thinking of the abrupt transition I had just passed through and I had a rare glimpse of things from what I believe was an eternal perspective. Mouzon Biggs had said at Bob's funeral that when Bob had first come to see him, he had asked, "Why is it that everyone I touch I hurt?" Then he went on to say that by the end of Bob's life, his touch had become a healing one. As I reflected on that comparison, I realized how true it was and that the dramatic transformation had taken place over the last couple of years of his life. He always said he was living on borrowed time. Once he ran into an acquaintance whom he hadn't seen in a long time, who said to him, with extraordinary tact, "Bob, what are you doing here; I thought you were dead." He told me later, "You know, I really should be dead." I blew that off as crazy talk, but I think now he was closer to the truth than I was. I thought of him asking in the hospital after his heart attack how anything good could come out of such a calamity. It seemed to me that the Lord said to Himself, "Here is a fellow with a teachable spirit. I'm going to give him a few more years and show him—and a lot of other people—what I can do." Taking away his desire to smoke was just the beginning. Next, he put his Spirit in him and used him right and left to change people's lives and put them in touch with Himself. It was a gem of an operation that the Lord pulled off.

Then I realized that I had been a significant part of that operation. I had known all along that God brought Bob and me together, but reflecting on having been chosen to participate in such a significant divine project made me profoundly and humbly conscious of the fact that God *knew* me. He knew I was a helper *meet* (suitable) for Bob. I *was* right for him. Through no merit of my own, but by God's grace, I understood the spiritual side of Bob. We were able to function as a team because we had a common vision of reality, even though everything was not always perfect between us. In addition, God knew I could adjust to losing him after just one year. I had been forced to face the issues of life and death and knew how to continue living after losing a husband.

At the same time, He knew of my need for a husband and of Glenn's for a father at this particular time, and He had managed to work all of that together for good through our short marriage. Here was that "divine alchemy" written about by Catherine Marshall clearly at work. Such knowledge, as the Psalmist wrote, is too wonderful for me.

These revelations that came to me as I lay on my bed that summer afternoon helped me put my life with Bob in perspective. I saw my marriage to him as a calling—a ministry—and somehow I felt I had done an acceptable job. I don't mean that I had done everything perfectly. There were many things I should have done differently. But I was obedient. The Lord had trusted me to do a job for Him, and he was pleased with me. There have been few times when I have been so conscious of God's love for me as I was that day.

Recognizing my marriage as a calling helped me understand my initial reaction when it became apparent that Bob was not going to be resuscitated after his heart attack. It was one of relief. "It's over," I had said to myself with the feeling of having lost a heavy burden. I didn't like myself for reacting that way and tried to deny it. Within the context of God's acceptance and affirmation that I felt so keenly that day, I was able to admit that being married to Bob *had* been a struggle. It was fun and satisfying, and fulfilling, and a lot of other positive things, but it was a struggle. He had tremendous emotional needs. Then there were so many uncertainties, having to do primarily with the precarious state of his health and his frustration at being unable to find gainful employment. These were burdens to him too. When I so comfortably said to myself, "It's over," it was as much for Bob as for me.

Foremost in my mind had been the fact that he would not have to go through another convalescence. He had been so gallant, getting up after every setback and continuing to fight, long after most of us would have given up. But to have to go back to square one would have been just too much. I couldn't bear to see him experience as much discouragement as that would have brought him. In light of this realization, I saw his death as the work of the mercy of God and it was right for me to be glad in it. During our year together, I had worried about the possibility of his death, especially at times when he failed to come home at an expected hour, and feared it as an unthinkable disaster. Now my worst fears had come to pass and it was all right. That special grace God gives to the needy was in evidence.

Teaching the Human Potential Class became a new calling. I spent hours studying for each lesson. Regretfully, I hadn't learned at that point that the most appropriate subject for any Sunday School class is the Bible. My lessons were essentially reviews of books by Christian writers, who often had a lot to say about the Bible, so I got at the truth that way, but it was not first hand. Nevertheless, people were very kind and indicated that they were helped by the lessons. One thing is sure, I was helped by preparing them and by the accepting response of the class. Their love upheld me through those awkward months of transition.

They helped me in practical ways as well. Jim Robinson took care of all manner of business matters for me, advised me on car care, and devoted many evenings to helping Glenn with Cub Scout projects. When I decided to economize by moving into a smaller apartment, half the class came on a Sunday afternoon and moved me, lock, stock, and barrel (and piano).

Later, when I did some traveling, they baby sat, as did some friends I met at a neighborhood Bible study. They showed me in a most concrete way what it means to bear one another's burdens. I still have a lot to learn in turning my attention away from my own business and addressing the needs of others.

During his earthly ministry, Jesus used parables to make spiritual truths clear. I think He used the experience of Bob's passing as a parable to teach me something about heaven. I was so apprehensive about leaving the warmth and familiarity of Laity Lodge and facing dear-knows-what back in Houston. I knew that dread was unfounded when Jean and John came running out of the back door to greet us when we arrived at my apartment. And I found the place full of people who loved me and were there to help in any way. It was overwhelming. If God's people function so exquisitely here on earth, can we expect any less in heaven? I think my homecoming was a shadow of the greeting that awaited Bob when he went home. The kingdom extends into this world and the next. If we like the communion of saints on this side, we'll love it over there! Until each of us makes that final trip, it's good to know we can experience something of heaven on earth by living our Christian life in community with other believers. I had many questions about the future, but I knew, as I had never known before, that I didn't have to face it alone.

12

What Do You Want Me To Do For You?

By the time I was forty years old, I had loved and lost two husbands. Those marriages were very different, but they shared at least one thing in common: each came about as a complete surprise to me. I have spent my share of time and energy looking for a husband, but each time one has appeared on the scene, I had nothing to do with it. I think there's a lesson there for anyone desiring to get married. In my experience, God has been able to do his matchmaking when I wasn't trying to help him. I had no idea after

Bob died that another such surprise was in store for me in the foreseeable future. Without thought of that possibility, I proceeded to set goals for establishing an appropriate framework of living for my existing family of two.

It seemed to me that the first requirement was to finish the academic degree in which I had already invested so many hours and dollars. I didn't know why I needed a PhD (I still don't), but there is something in me that won't rest until I've completed a job once started. (I'm feeling that compulsion right now with this book.) It probably has something to do with the puritan ethic, which has been much maligned in recent history, but which figured prominently in my upbringing and I believe in it, 'though I don't do a masterful job of applying it. At any rate, to that end, I resigned from my teaching job in order to devote the year to writing a dissertation. It was a good move. Besides accomplishing its primary purpose, it made unstructured time available for me to spend with Glenn and to prepare Sunday school lessons. Later, when opportunities arose for me to participate in various renewal conferences, I was free to travel.

The first trip I took was back to Laity Lodge when the Human Potential Class went there in September for a retreat. We traveled by chartered bus and were told when we arrived that ours was the first bus ever to descend into the canyon and ford the river. The trip was marked by much hilarity, but walking into the Great Hall and seeing the couch where Bob had died was sobering for me. I was glad to be surrounded by people who shared my sense of loss.

The director of Laity Lodge, Bill Cody, had invited Creath Davis, a minister from Dallas, to serve as resource person. Creath was a deeply spiritual man with an infectious sense of humor and was perfect for us. I learned from his teaching about the woman at the well in John 4 that Jesus not only loves us, he *likes* us. It was a powerful new revelation.

In a private conversation with Creath, I shared my concern about Glenn. I worried about his lack of a father and was afraid this might hinder the development of his identity as a man. His answer was one of the most encouraging things I've ever been told. He told me of a friend of his who had lost his father at a very young age who had become a wonderful father to his own children. It seemed that being deprived of his own father somehow made him more appreciative of the role and enabled him to do a better job. It turned my thinking on the subject inside out.

A poignant sequel to this encounter occurred many years later. One August morning I tuned in to James Dobson's "Focus on the Family" radio broadcast in midstream as he was telling about speaking at a memorial service for four friends who had died in a plane crash. When he referred to "Pastor Creath", I came to attention. "Could that be Creath Davis?" I thought, whereupon Dr. Dobson said, "Who could fail to love Creath Davis?" Then I knew Creath was indeed one of those being eulogized. I was so moved that I sat right down and wrote Dr. Dobson a letter telling of Creath's impact on my life, as a kind of memorial, I said, and asked him to pass my remarks on to the families involved. Several months later, I heard from the wife of one of the other victims of the crash. Ann Clark wrote to tell me her husband, George, was undoubtedly the person Creath had told me about who had grown up with no father and was enabled later to be such a good father. She marveled, as I do, at how God used the example of George to encourage me in a time of need, and then years later turned around and used me to minister to her. As she wrote in her letter, God is indeed a God of details. And I would add that being a part of His network—his communion of saints—is a privilege almost too good to be true.

In April of 1974, I journeyed to Stony Point, New York, to attend a week-long Leadership Training Institute sponsored by Faith-at-Work. As part of our training, we were given an assignment to take a portion of scripture and write a relational Bible study about it. In leading such a study, one first shares where he sees himself in the particular passage and what that indicates about the current stage of his spiritual pilgrimage. Then questions are designed to help others find insights about their own lives in relation to the scripture. I chose the account in Luke 18:35-43 about the blind beggar who asked Jesus to restore his sight. His request came in response to Jesus' question, "What do you want me to do for you?" Those words jumped out at me. It was as if Jesus were standing there asking me that question: "Marianne, what do you want me to do for you?" I didn't have to ponder the question. I knew immediately that what I wanted in my heart of hearts was to be married again. This didn't seem quite proper, considering that Bob had not been gone so much as a year, but I told the Lord anyway that this was my deepest desire. When I shared it later with my small group, they were most affirming and joined me in committing the matter to the Lord.

The idea of marriage remained so committed that I didn't give it another thought when I went home and got caught up in rapidly moving events. I had given up my job believing that a new job would materialize when it was time for me to go back to work. I couldn't envision what this might be. I knew I couldn't go back into classroom teaching—I just didn't have it in me to do that anymore—and I wasn't really interested in moving to some far away place to teach in college, which seemed to be the only thing my training was preparing me for. To say I experienced stress during the spring is a gross understatement.

At one point, I went into a black depression. There seemed to be no possibility of suitable employment. On one of my darkest days, two friends who proved to be no less than angels, Stan and Mary Rodgers, came and took me to lunch. I remember looking at the lovely houses in the subdivision in Stafford, south of Houston, where Stan was a homebuilder and pitying myself because I would never have a home of my own. I don't know what they said to lift my spirits, but I remember laughing a lot over lunch. Soon afterward, the answer to my dilemma came, as usual, in an unexpected way.

Early one morning my telephone rang and it was a new friend, Cleone Ashton. We had met at a Cub Scout pack meeting and had discovered that we both had worked for Miss DuBois in the Music Department at the University of Texas. We immediately found large areas of common interest, ranging from our sons to our vocations. She called to tell me that the Spring Branch school board had voted the night before to add music specialists in their elementary schools and she thought I might be interested. The lights went on. I knew this was what I had been waiting for.

I filed an application forthwith with the school district, and within a few days was thrilled to receive in the mail one of those big white envelopes stamped *CONTRACT ENCLOSED.* I've never figured out why I needed a PhD to be an elementary school music teacher, but that has been my profession for fifteen years and I've never questioned that it is the right one for me. Even with all the pressures and frustrations of teaching in today's public schools—and they increase every year—I still find it fulfilling and enriching. (I would like it better if it didn't consume so much of my energy that the rest of my life is usually out of control.)

Amidst all this trauma, I managed to get my dissertation written, approved, typed, and submitted, passed the oral examination, and had the satisfaction of walking across the platform at graduation to be hooded. I'm glad I went through the ceremony, because I've never had occasion to wear that hood since.

One Sunday night, sitting propped up in bed reading the *Houston Post*, I received the impetus for another important move in my life. A friend at church was looking for a house, and I was browsing through the housing section to see if I could see something she might like when it suddenly dawned on me that there was no reason why I couldn't buy a house, now that, at long last, I had a guaranteed income. I saw prices quoted for houses on the far west side of Houston that seemed to be compatible with my budget. The next morning I drove out Interstate 10 to a subdivision rising out of a rice field near the little town of Katy and really liked the atmosphere there. Later, my homebuilder friend, Stan, went there with me and guided me through the process of selecting, getting a loan for, and buying a little house suitable for Glenn and me. I know that without his managing the transaction I would never have been able to pull it off.

We moved in June, and I was so grateful to be under my own roof. I remember sitting on the sofa in the den one morning looking out the bare window at the treeless, weed-covered back yard and thanking God for giving us stability with a house and a job. We had fun working to turn the house into a home. Glenn helped me dig flower beds, and I looked forward to Fridays when the nursery advertisements came out in the paper. I bought and planted whatever was on sale, which always included pine trees. All those eighty-eight cent seedlings are a forest today.

We had never lived in a house with a fireplace, so when the weather turned cold we had great fun with the fire. Some nights we slept in the den with the fire burning. It reminded me of nights I spent with my grandmother as a child when I watched the coal fire flicker after we turned off the light. I could almost smell the Mentholatum she used. Glenn slept on the love seat and I slept on the sofa. If we did it today, we'd have to swap places, as he is the big one now.

It was such a blessing to have my life on an even keel after so much change and emotional turmoil over the past several years. I was thoroughly content and decided to devote the following years, while Glenn was still at home, to raising him. Another marriage could come when he was grown. As usual, things didn't turn out as I planned.

One Wednesday night at the sharing group, which was still meeting in the church downtown, I was introduced to a man named Horace Smith. We soon discovered much in common, mostly related to the fact that we are nearly the same age (he lived for a short time under Herbert Hoover before I came along with FDR), and we both majored in music in college. We became good friends, but that didn't keep me from feeling slightly insulted when he left in the middle of my Sunday school lessons to go and direct his choir. He sang in the choir at the early service at First Methodist, then drove across town to direct for the 11:00 service at another church. He also sang in the Houston Symphony Chorale.

Once he invited me to go with him to an event sponsored by the Chorale. It was called a "Sing", to which people bought tickets to sing major choral works with an orchestra of Houston Symphony players. Such an event was most appealing to me, so I accepted, even though I had decided not to get involved in dating at that time. As expected, I loved the event. We read through great choruses by such composers as Bach, Handel, Mozart, and Beethoven. It was also pleasant being with Horace.

One Sunday morning I had the television tuned to the channel that carried the early service at First Methodist and happened to walk through the den just as the choir processed in. I spotted the back of Horace's head with its bald spot and got the funniest little feeling of tenderness and fascination. (I know this sounds ridiculous, but I had never paid any attention to baldness in men before.) Later the choir sang "The Heavens are Telling" from Haydn's *Creation*, and Horace sang the part of Uriel in the trio. As I watched and listened, those feelings of tenderness intensified. "What is going on?" I thought, and dismissed the incident as adolescent-style fantasy. From time to time in the days that followed, the thought of our being more than just friends crossed my mind, but I continued to dismiss the possibility. It didn't fit my plan, and besides, Horace had indicated no such interest in me.

A short time afterward, he asked me out again and I went. At the end of the evening we were sitting on the couch having a normal conversation when, out of the blue, he asked me to marry him. You could have knocked me over with a feather. "You're kidding!" I answered. It didn't come out the way I meant it. I was thinking, "How did you know thoughts along that line have been flitting in and out of my mind? I thought I had kept them secret." Without the slightest hint of a flinch at my flippant reply, he said, "No—I'll love you and cherish you for the rest of my life."

This changed the whole landscape for me. I saw a man willing to risk insult and rejection and laying his very soul out for me. It was something to take very seriously and consider carefully. I looked at him for a long time thinking how like my father he was in his guileless vulnerability. Finally I said thoughtfully, "It might work." I was going to have to take another look at my long range plans.

I may not be the smartest person in the world, but I'm no dummy. My first thought was that you don't find a good man like Horace standing on every corner. The magnanimity of his proposal had spoken volumes to me about his character. I was not as worldly-wise as I might have been, but I had been around enough to know that an old song speaks the truth: *A Good Man Nowadays Is Hard to Find.* I had found one, and wonder of wonders, he said he loved me.

Then I recognized that Horace is one of the most accepting people I've ever met, which would go a long way toward making a life shared with him a happy one. Those who know him would be quick to point out that there are some things about which he is hopelessly intolerant, such as bad singing (incorrect vocal technique) and "inferior" music, especially in church, but he was amazingly tolerant of me and my shortcomings. And he accepted Glenn. I could see that he would be a friend and adviser to him rather than a strong disciplinarian, and my intuition, which seems to have been right, told me this was just the kind of dad Glenn needed at that point.

All these things plus the fact that I just thought he would be fun to live with led me to give Horace an affirmative answer, and we set a date for the Wednesday of my week-long spring break. On March 26, 1975, two days after my forty-second birthday, the minister of music at Houston's First Methodist Church,

Roger Deschner, performed the marriage ceremony in the recently renovated and exceptionally lovely chapel there. The Wednesday night sharing group was a captive audience, and they were joined by local and out-of-town friends. In place of my father, who had passed away two years before, my friend Hal Haralson came from Austin and gave me away. Hal and I had met on the airplane on the way to the conference at Stony Point, and our friendship continued to grow when we were in the same small group there. Also coming from Austin were Russell and Susanne Schulz. My roommate from L. S. U., Peggy Lane, surprised me by coming in from Kansas City. She had been there for my last wedding, as had the Schulzes, and I told them I hoped they wouldn't have to come to any more of my weddings. My sisters came from Jackson.

After the recessional, we all boarded the elevators and went up to the fifth floor for a reception. This arrangement was not original with this wedding. We had gotten so good at putting on receptions in the fifth floor parlor that we jokingly called ourselves the Human Potential Catering Service.

When I told the Lord at Stony Point that I would like to be married, I didn't expect him to bring it about within a year. I was thinking more in terms of a decade. But He knew something I didn't know—that the cozy, under-control, peaceful state of affairs I was so comfortable with was, like every stage in life, a passing phenomenon. Challenges and pressures lay ahead that would cause me to draw heavily on Horace's strength and generosity of spirit. Taking him up on his proposal was a good decision. And he *has* been fun to live with! (I'm happy to report that he agrees, even after all these years of putting up with me.)

13

A Lamp Unto My Feet

The fourteenth chapter of the Second Book of Chronicles describes the reign of King Asa of Judah in phrases that could apply to the next period of my life:

> the kingdom was quiet before him;
> the land had rest, and he had no war in those years;
> because the LORD had given him rest. and he hath given us rest on every side.[1]

With my marriage to Horace I entered into a time of peace and security with no battles to fight or big problems to solve. I simply delighted in family living.

---

[1] II Chronicles 14:5-7.

Shortly after we were married, we attended a sports event sponsored by Glenn's elementary school. Sitting with Horace on the bleachers in an antiquated gymnasium in Katy, I basked in the delight of being a family. For the first time, that part of my life was complete.

As unconcerned as I usually am about athletics, attending sports events became symbolic of being an ordinary family, and these became a regular part of our routine. We bought season tickets to watch the Katy Tigers play football every Friday night. The school district had not yet built its modern state-of-the-art stadium, and games were played on a field behind the high school in an atmosphere much like what I remembered of Leland. Horace attempted to explain to me what was happening on the field while Glenn roamed around visiting with his friends and watching the band. He had loved the trombone since I took him to outdoor concerts by the University of Texas Concert Band when he was a little boy, and when he started band in sixth grade, that was his instrument. In the years ahead, band concerts and contests would be added to ball games for our family excursions.

To further identify with our community, we decided to transfer our membership from the church in downtown Houston to the First United Methodist Church in Katy, where we were warmly welcomed and soon felt we belonged. We sang in the choir and participated in a weekly sharing group. We loved the church and would not have left it but for the fact that Horace had an opportunity to direct a choir in another church.

During this time of rest, a long-dormant gift of mine began to stir. The last time I had seriously played the piano was in those distant days in Del Rio when Helen

Lamp Unto My Feet 161

Doering and I performed duo-piano music. In the years since, I had been busy with other things and had touched the piano only occasionally, just to play, never to practice. One day at school our fifth graders were in the cafetorium practicing for a bicentenniel musical. The other music teacher, Margaret Peterson, was directing and I was at the piano. As I sight-read the catchy accompaniments for each number, it struck me how remarkable it was that someone could look at those black marks on a page and translate them into live music. I was suddenly very grateful for the gift of being able to do that, and to do it fairly well. I remember telling myself that I should be using that ability instead of allowing it grow rusty and stiff under a bushel, as I had for well over a dozen years. Those thoughts seemed like idle mind-wanderings at the time, but in light of subsequent events, I think they may have been the still, small voice of the Spirit telling me to get ready to start doing a lot more playing.

One day a portable sign appeared at the Mason Road exit off Interstate 10, where we live, announcing that a new Methodist church was being formed and inviting interested people to attend an organizational meeting. We joined a handful of people on the appointed Sunday morning at an elementary school, where the district superintendent, Dr. Rankin, told us the new church would be called St. Peter's United Methodist Church. Horace volunteered to lead the singing, which seemed to be appreciated. When someone donated a little organ with no pedals but with numerous switches to produce (not necessarily appropriate) sound effects, I offered to play the hymns. The instrument worked fine except one morning when I accidentally hit a switch that gave a "ch" sound to every chord. "Holy, Holy, Holy" never sounded with so much pizzazz. I didn't know when I casually started playing hymns for those informal services that I was embarking upon a career in church music ministry that would continue to grow to this day. Over the years, the church acquired progressively larger organs, with which my ability to play grew. Horace organized a choir, meeting first in our living room, then in the church office in a shopping center before a building was constructed. When we left there to take over the music at the local Episcopal Church, that smattering of souls that began meeting in a school gymnasium had grown to more than one thousand in membership. (Actually, I left to retire from the organ bench, but it wasn't long before Horace had me at it again.)

Those years were a wonderful gift—a time to savor the little everyday joys of living, for which I thanked God regularly. There is a time to rest, and a time to move forward, as the writer of the Book of Ecclesiastes might have expressed it. This is especially true of the spiritual life, and when the Lord is ready for me to grow in the knowledge of Him, he usually sends along circumstances I can't control. (That is, circumstances I *know* I can't control; I can't control any of them, but sometimes I think I can.) These, in turn, drive me into His arms. This happened to me in an unusual way about five years into this period of my life.

One of the benefits of that peaceful interlude was that I read a number of secular books. Herman Wouk's sweeping novels built around World War II and events leading up to it, *The Winds of War* and *War and Remembrance*, left deep impressions that made the movie versions seem shallow in comparison. I think that is because the printed version lends itself to much pondering between the lines. I pondered many things in the course of reading those monumental sagas, but I was especially struck by the strength and stature of the

United States during that period of history. And I thought how I had been blessed to grow up in the security of the strongest country in the world.

Later I read Theodore White's account of his journalistic career, *In Search of History*. He began his career the year I was born, so I interpreted the events he chronicled against the background of the years of my life, which was most enlightening. His eyewitness account of the ceremony of Japanese surrender aboard the *USS Missouri* in Tokyo Bay blew me away. He told of the assemblage of witnesses packed on the ship's deck, where each person was allotted "two square feet of tiptoe space"; the delegation of commanding officers from each branch of the service; and, of course, the press. The eleven Japanese representatives were the last to appear before General McArthur emerged to conduct the ceremony. He read his prepared remarks from a paper held in quivering hands, expressing his hope that out of the carnage of the past a better world would emerge—"a world founded upon faith and understanding—a world dedicated to the dignity of man and the fulfillment of his most cherished wish—for freedom, tolerance, and justice"—and announcing his plans to discharge his responsibilities with justice and tolerance. He then looked directly at the Japanese, saying "I now invite the representatives of the Emperor of Japan and the Japanese Government, and the Japanese Imperial General Headquarters to sign the instrument of surrender at the places indicated." I could virtually feel the hush of suspended time as the two Japanese signed the document, one sitting in a chair, the other bending over from the waist. The next event must be told in White's own words:

It was as Umezu straightened again that the last thing happened—and happened to the split second in the perfect timing of the victorious forces we then commanded. The rain of Saturday had ended, the skies were lightening, and now the clouds above the ship were breaking with sun patches when a drone sounded. It began as a light buzzing in the distance, then a roar, then the deafening tone of countless planes converging. Four hundred B-29's, the fire bombers that had leveled Japan, had taken off from Guam and Saipan hours before; the fleet carriers had coordinated their planes. They were to appear over the *Missouri* all at once. And they did. The four hundred B-29's came low, low over the *Missouri*, and fifteen hundred fleet planes rose above and around their wings. There they were, speckling the sky in flecks of scudding gray; it was American power at zenith. They dipped over the *Missouri*, passed on over Yokohama, inland over Tokyo to brandish the threat, then back out to sea again.[2]

This paragraph, written by a master reporter, gives us a breathtaking snapshot of an awesome moment in world history—the preeminent nation in the world accepting the surrender of a formidable enemy who seemed at the time to be our last enemy. In it, the ceremony is played out with the dignity, flare, and symbolism that only a man like General McArthur could arrange. The last scene of his account no doubt moved me to the point of remembering it long after forgetting other details of the book because I identified with another generation of those flyers; but the scene also represented to me the epitome of America's military might and political power. The remaining two-thirds of the book reflects a decline from the heights described here.

---

[2] Theodore H. White, *In Search of History* (New York: Harper & Row, 1978), pp. 239-240.

At about the time I finished reading it, a group of Iranian "students" stormed the U. S. Embassy in Teheran, taking dozens of hostages, and it soon became apparent that we were powerless to do anything about it. An ongoing television news program called "America Held Hostage" was beamed into the living rooms of America every night. There were no lights on the White House Christmas tree that year. I was one American who suffered an uncomfortable sense of foreboding.

One morning early in the new year, the news on Houston's classical music station that daily awakens Horace and me told of Russian tanks rolling into Afghanistan. I was struck with terror. If we couldn't get our own embassy back from a gang of fanatical religious zealots in Iran, what could we do if the Russians decided to roll those tanks any place they chose? The safety we had enjoyed in America for my whole life because of our unquestioned strength was threatened and could no longer be taken for granted.

When I saw Afghanistan on the map, I realized that if the Russians kept moving south they would eventually reach Israel, and I remembered something Macky told us at Camp Merri-Mac in 1950. My training in Bible prophecy was sketchy at best. I first heard about the "end of the world" from an ancient black lady who took care of the baby in our family when I was a child. Her version of what to expect at the consummation of history was enough to cause me to avoid the subject, but Macky's remark stuck with me. She told us that Israel had just recently been established as a Jewish nation, just as the scriptures had foretold, and that we could expect the Lord's return any time; and she told us to watch the Middle East, because events associated with the end of the age would unfold there. All that seemed so remote and unlikely (and scary) that I hadn't given it a thought since. With the latest turn of events, however, I was suddenly very interested. I wanted to find out what the Bible has to say about the end times, because it seemed as if we might be approaching them.

One morning while driving to work, I happened to tune into a radio program called "A Roundtable on Revelation", which immediately got my attention. The important thing about that was that it introduced me to Christian radio. I felt as if I had discovered a hidden treasure. I began to listen to that station every chance I had and at first gave equal credence to everything I heard. Eventually my attention narrowed to a few expository Bible teachers and I drank in their broadcasts like a sponge. Soon, instead of trying to learn just about prophecy, I wanted to learn about God himself, and the teachers I heard taught about Him in a way I had never heard.

At about that time, a friend I had known when I went to Houston's First Methodist Church, Linda Jones, invited me to a visitors night at a Bible study pilot program she had participated in during the summer. We were given an opportunity there to enroll in a new night class sponsored by Bible Study Fellowship, an international teaching ministry. In September I began their year-long study of the Book of Genesis. After years of groping around in the dark trying to live the Christian life, I began at that point to become biblically literate and to use the Word of God as a source of truth and direction. For the next five years, Tuesday evening was reserved for Bible Study Fellowship.

My attitude toward the Bible was turned around early in the Genesis study. The teaching leader showed on a screen a diagram of a time-line of history from the creation to the Lord's second coming. At a point between the beginning and the end was a drawing of a cross, dominating the scene. As the saying goes, a picture is worth a thousand words, and that one spoke volumes to me. It struck me that we live in the same time continuum into which Jesus came, God invading human history. And I knew as I studied that diagram that Adam also lived in the same continuum. I had come to believe long before that Jesus Christ was the Son of God and that He came to take away our sins, but I was still infected (or vaccinated?) with what my mother calls the "take it with a grain of salt" school of theology. That is the view of the Bible that maintains that it's true, but it's not true. All those things the Bible tells about didn't necessarily happen as they are recorded in its pages, but that doesn't matter because there is still truth there, a "kernel of truth". I never articulated this view; rather, it was an unspoken underlying assumption. But the night I looked at that time line, with its cross tow'ring o'er the wrecks of time, I knew the Bible was true from start to finish. I'm not prepared to argue this with a theologian, but I know that when I began to take the Word of God at face value, believing that it means what it says, it began to make sense to me in a way it never had before.

One of the most helpful parts of Bible Study Fellowship is the sheet of questions to be answered on each lesson before it is covered in class. The questions are carefully planned to lead the student to reach conclusions on his own. I was amazed at the insights I got just from answering questions on a passage, before hearing any discussion or lecture on it. When we studied Adam's fall in Genesis 3, the proverbial light bulb turned on in my head when I realized that God made clothes for Adam and Eve out of animal skins because it was necessary that something die in order that their sin be covered. Then I understood why Jesus died on the cross. I had heard since childhood, and believed, that Jesus died to take away my sins, but this was the first time I understood why it was necessary that he do it.

On one of those Tuesdays, the Lord showed me that He could speak to me personally through His word. I had heard people tell about hearing directly from the Lord through specific passages of scripture, and I thought that could never happen to me—I was not that spiritual. During the break that night between the discussion time and the lecture, I was standing in line in the restroom worried sick over Glenn. He had just reached the magic age of sixteen and had a brand new driver's license. We had bought him a pre-owned Volkswagen Scirroco out of necessity, as the three of us in the family always seemed to be going in different directions. Such was the case on this Tuesday night. Horace was in downtown Houston at a symphony chorale rehearsal; I was at Bible Study Fellowship; and Glenn was at his job at K-Mart. The store was about ten miles up the interstate from our house, and I held my breath every time he made the trip. Turning my little boy out on the freeway by himself was just too much. My mind was working overtime producing "what-ifs". The big one was "What if some calamity happened and Glenn needed us when no one was home?" Just as my turn in line came and I shut myself in the privacy of the cubicle, I said, "Lord, you talk to all these other people; give me a scripture to take away this crazy fear." At that moment the refrain of a song I didn't even know I knew popped into my mind: *For I know whom I have believed, and am persuaded that He is able to keep that which I've committed unto Him against that day.*

I was awed. The Lord knew me, a little old insignificant school teacher in Houston, Texas, and had gone to the trouble to answer my heart cry. He knew that scripture was tucked away in my mind, clothed in an ignoble little tune beginning with an octave leap, and he spoke directly to me through it. Of course He was able to keep what I had committed to Him, and I had committed Glenn to Him many times. He was telling me He would take care of him. Regrettably, that wasn't the last time I would find myself tied in knots of worry about Glenn. God has reminded me with that same verse many times since then that He is in control (slow learner that I am). Just as I knew years before that He was in control of my first husband, I had to include in that control any outcome the Lord might allow. Faith is not believing some specific thing; it is believing that God has the interests of His children at heart and that He will work out all things for their eternal good. And if He says he's in control, he's in control. That word, coming to me in such a dramatic way, was welcome news indeed.

I learned some important things from that incident. One was that we are limited in our ability to hear from God by paucity of knowledge of His word. That is, the more of His word we know, the more the Lord is able to illuminate that word in specific circumstances of our lives. I had received what I believe to be direct communications from Him in the past, but never with the certainty that comes through His written word. Also, it must surely be easier for Him to get through to us when we open ourselves to the word He has already given us in scripture so that He has something to work with. This makes Bible study of primary importance, not just something that is nice to do when we have time, and it is certainly more than mere self-improvement.

The second lesson I learned is the efficacy of music to implant the word in one's mind. I don't even know where I learned that musical rendition of II Timothy 1:12 that came to me that night in the rest room. It is not in any of the hymnals I grew up with; but somewhere I sang it, and with the remembrance of the tune came the words. Finding ways to help people learn the Word of God through music would occupy much of my attention in the future.

I fell in love with the Lord Jesus—the living Word—early in my spiritual pilgrimage. Now I had fallen in love with His Word—the written Word—as well. No longer would I be a scrawny, malnourished Christian. I had discovered what Peter calls the *pure milk of the word that I might grow thereby.*[3] And through that word I learned that the ultimate source of security is not in living in a strong country but in the Lord himself: *Some trust in chariots, and some in horses; but we will remember the name of the LORD our God."*[4]

---

[3] I Peter 2:2.
[4] Psalm 20:7.

14

Peter, Go Ring the Bells

*I wonder where my brother has gone,
wonder where my brother has gone,
wonder where my brother has gone,
I heard from heaven to day.*

*O Peter, go ring the bells,
Peter, go ring the bells,
Peter, go ring the bells
I heard from heaven today.*
(American Spiritual)

On September 1, 1939, German troops marched into Poland from three sides, thereby starting World War II. I read about it in history books later. When it happened, I was concerned with other things. On that day, my little sister, Corinne, and I took a trip with our father to the other side of the Delta. It must have been that day, because on the last day of August, my mother had given birth to a bouncing baby boy in the hospital in Greenwood, and Daddy took us to see him. Riding along in the back seat of our black 2-door Ford, Corinne and I entertained ourselves trying out names for our new little brother. His name was Leo, but we couldn't call him that; that was Daddy's name. We really laughed when one of us suggested "Butter". The one that stuck was "Bubba". For the rest of his life, Francis Leo Gerdes, Jr., was known as Bubba. (Daddy may have figured out from his Catholic upbringing that he was named for a saint and a pope, but I bet Bubba never knew!) We have home movies taken a few days later of my pretty young mother standing at the front door holding the baby and waving to me as I skipped down the walk with my hair in pigtails and carrying a bright plaid book satchel on my way to my first day at Leland Elementary School.

Forty-seven years later, I was in another elementary school when I received a telephone call telling me that my little brother was dead. I wasn't ready for that. I had thought of the possibility of losing other people close to me, but never one of my siblings. After all, I was the oldest. They would lose me some day, but I should never have to face losing one of them. In the shock of hearing that Bubba was gone, our whole life together flashed before my mind.

I remembered how I loved him when he was a baby. Mama used to let him lie down for a while with Corinne and me after we went to bed, and when she came and got him, I was careful not to disturb the imprint left by his little head in the feather pillow. As he grew up, it was almost impossible to get him to go to sleep at night. After another baby, Rachel, came along, it became my job to lie down with Bubba until he went to sleep. I would lie as still as a statue for what seemed like hours, thinking of the homework and piano practicing I should be doing. When I thought he was asleep, I would carefully move one muscle at a time in slipping out. Sometimes I was too early, and he would ask in his husky little voice, "Where you going?" Then I would have to start all over again and the clock ticked on. I don't remember complaining about the job. I liked being with him.

He was always bad. Not mean, just bad—like when he discovered I was squeamish about dead mice. Then he unmercifully chased me around the house dangling the victim of a mousetrap by its tail. His fourth grade teacher loves to tell the story of the time he was accused of calling a little girl a "bow-legged jackass." He defended himself, saying "No, Ma'am, I did *not* say she was bowlegged."

Once when I was in high school, I was dressed for a dance in an ice blue satin formal with a bustle in which two artificial roses were embedded. Just as I stepped out the front door with my date, Bubba came along with a knife and cut off one of those roses. I remember laughing, not getting mad. He was so cute.

And he was smart, and talented, and funny. When he was in high school, he regaled audiences with his rendition of a piece, popularized by Andy Griffith, about a country bumpkin's first visit to a football game. Later, he could keep a crowd's attention playing his guitar and singing country songs. He even wrote some songs and made one record. When he finished college, he could have done anything he wanted to do, but something else had hold of him that would keep him from reaching any of his goals.

I don't know when he started drinking, but he used to call us in Del Rio when he was well under the influence of alcohol. He was about twenty then. My husband, Glenn, told me not to worry, that he would outgrow it; but even then I had an uneasy feeling that it was more serious than that. I was right. In the years that followed, his drinking went from bad to worse. When I met my second husband, Bob, and learned about AA, I sent Bubba a little pamphlet listing indicators of a drinking problem. He sent it back with a colorful note telling me what to do with it. That was obviously the wrong approach. The tragedy is that he never availed himself of any help. As a result, we virtually lost touch, except for some middle-of-the-night telephone conversations, for about ten years.

Then one Good Friday afternoon, I had the television tuned to a Christian talk show out of Canada while I was frantically trying to finish a dress in time to wear on Easter. (I haven't outgrown the notion that you need new clothes for Easter; I hope the reason has more to do with symbolism than vanity.) Over the hum of the sewing machine, I heard someone on the program quote Isaiah 58:7, ending with "...and not to turn away from your own flesh and blood," and I was convicted. That is exactly what I had done. Those endless, repetitious late night phone calls were so wearing I had gradually cut myself off from Bubba altogether.

Our acquaintance was renewed a short time later when he started doing business in south Texas and was able to stop by for visits with us from time to time. I loved discovering my brother again. We had many good times together, laughing a lot. You couldn't be with Bubba without laughing. He started calling me during the day and we laughed some more. We also talked seriously. He realized that he had missed some opportunities in the past and told me mistakes he felt he had made. I always assured him that it was not too late to start over. It seemed to me that he was taking a healthy look at his life up to that point and was about to change directions. He even said he realized that he just couldn't drink, as if that were a surprising discovery. He thought he could control it by himself and wasn't interested in seeking help.

Once he visited us on Thanksgiving. We had joined the Episcopal Church by then and I was playing the organ for the service that morning. I timidly asked him to go, thinking it was something he wouldn't want to do. I was wrong. Using the name he and Corinne had always called me, he said, "Di'e, you don't ever have to apologize about taking me to church." We all went—Horace, Glenn (who adored his uncle), Bubba and I. Our priest, Tony Tripi, preached a good sermon about being thankful in everything. When the peace was exchanged, Bubba gregariously introduced himself to those around him and was about to leave when everyone sat down for the offertory and communion service. In the churches we were familiar with, people greeted each other at the end of the service, not in the middle. We laughed a little about that. It wasn't the first time we had laughed in church. Once in Leland we made the pew shake when a man at communion missed the kneeling rail and landed on the floor, setting us off. As far as I know, that Thanksgiving Day was the last time Bubba went to church. I don't think he forgot God, though. One of his friends, who drove eight hundred miles from south Texas to attend his funeral, told us Bubba traveled with a Bible next to his seat in his truck.

The next year, he came to see us for Christmas. He was late (he never showed up any place when he said he would) and made his appearance around supper time. My cousins, Bob Gerdes and Catherine Berninger, and friend, Linda Jones, were at our house. Earlier, all of us had enjoyed a sumptuous buffet at the Adams Mark Hotel and had come home to visit and let all the food we had eaten settle. Bubba walked in like Santa Claus in a red plaid shirt with red suspenders. After a while, he started playing Glenn's guitar and singing for us. I was in the kitchen getting some supper together (I couldn't believe we were hungry again) when I realized my living room was rocking. Bubba had turned it into a honkytonk with his music. It was funny because it was so incongruous. I have such a proper living room. We practically had to hold our sides from laughing so much. All of us except Horace, that is—he had surreptitiously slipped into the bedroom and probably had KUHF, the classical station, turned up full blast!

At bedtime, I was making up the hide-a-bed in my study when I heard Bubba, sounding for all the world like a little boy, playing the guitar and singing, "I took Jesus as my Savior, you take him too" Memory of that would be an immense comfort to me before the new year was gone.

I saw him one more time when he met me in April for Parents Weekend at Texas A&M. This was Glenn's senior year, and he had insisted that his Uncle Bubba come. I'm glad, because it was fun. We had dinner Saturday at a lively restaurant called Fajita Rita's. The next morning, Bubba and I were at the campus early for a special ceremony presented by Glenn's squadron in the Corps of Cadets. At lunch there was a bar-be-que. Early in the afternoon, he told me he had to go. Listening to the boys in the dorm talk about their plans for the future had reminded him of his lost opportunities and he was depressed. I assured him that people start over at all ages, and that it surely was not too late for him. That didn't seem to help, and I was sad for him. I watched him pull off in his big truck for the last time.

Bubba never met a stranger. He had the same open, unsuspicious demeanor that our father had. He liked people and expected them to like him, which, of course, made him vulnerable to insult and injury. On the other hand, like many people when they have too much to drink, he could be obnoxious. That, combined with his trusting nature, caused him to end up late one night with a bullet in his chest. And that's when I got a call at school telling me to come home.

Stark tragedy. Just when it seemed he was about to start getting his life together, he died an ignominious death. There seemed to be no possibility of comfort for those he left behind. That night, Glenn and I left from Hobby Airport for Mississippi on the saddest trip I ever took.

Comfort did come from the city of Leland and its environs as its inhabitants descended on my mother's house like angels of mercy. I felt it most at the funeral. I had chosen the music, which included two congregational hymns. I didn't want any soupy funeral music. I met my cousin and former teacher, Alice Kathryn Turner, at the church and we went over everything she would play. The opening hymn was "How Firm a Foundation". I thought in choosing it that since there seemed to be no comfort to hold on to, humanly speaking, at least we could hold on to Jesus. The minister instructed the family to remain seated while the congregation stood for the hymn. It's a good thing, because I don't think I could have stood up. When the church full of saints began to sing "How firm a foundation, ye saints of the Lord, Is laid for your faith in his excellent word..." to a sturdy tune called *Foundation*, which seems to move from one rock-anchored shaft to the next, I literally felt my spirit being lifted up. I tried to sing, but couldn't—the only time in my life I can remember being unable to sing. I let them do it for me. My mother and I clung to each other through the service, both remembering the day Bubba was brought to the left side of the altar before which his coffin stood to be baptized when he was a baby. And the communion of saints held us up.

There *was* some comfort. Everyone who came to the house after the funeral knew Bubba's weakness and shortcomings. But it was apparent that he left a reservoir of love among the people who knew him. Flowers came from people he did business with all over the south, and some of them drove long distances to come. Friends who came and friends who wrote spoke of his integrity and character. Some told of ways he had helped them when they needed it. One man, his friend since childhood, who had become involved in a white collar crime and spent some time in the Mississippi State Penitentiary, regaled us with an account of Bubba visiting him there. He told us about Bubba parking his truck near a fence around the facility and calling an inmate over to ask if his friend was there. The friend was fetched and said he looked up and there was Bubba, standing there in his big hat, bright shirt, jeans, and cowboy boots, laughing. They sat down for a long visit through the fence. *I was in prison and you visited me.*[1] How many of us who seem to have life so altogether have visited someone in prison?

These stories were comforting, but our feelings of guilt were not. My sisters and I were especially burdened by our failure to help Bubba more. At one point, someone said, through tears, "Bubba was such a needy person," and I agreed. It would have been so

---

[1] Matthew 25:36

much easier if we had known he was in heaven, but we didn't. The question of where his spirit went when his life was suddenly cut off continued to torment me in the weeks that followed.

Sitting in church one Sunday morning, I just dumped the whole thing in the Lord's lap. I said, "Lord, I know you don't want me to carry this kind of a burden. I can't handle it. Show me how I'm supposed to think about Bubba." A few nights later I was stepping out of the bathtub after a long time of soaking and thinking about Bubba, having just reached the conclusion that all those prayers I prayed for him surely had not been ignored, when it seemed to me that Bubba himself was speaking to me—not audibly, but in my head. I recognized the inflection in his voice when he seemed to say, "Di'e, it's all right over here." He always used the expression "all right" to mean he approved. He had told my mother that I was "all right" and I had taken it as a substantial compliment. I said, "Lord, is that message from you?" Somehow, I thought it was, but I wanted more indication than a thought, be it ever so vivid.

At that time, I read for my morning devotionals the readings for the Daily Office in the back of the *Book of Common Prayer*. I had found that nearly every day something in one of the readings spoke directly to a situation in my life. It made each morning exciting, because I knew there would be some message just for me. Usually these were in the Psalms. On the morning after I thought I had heard something about Bubba's whereabouts in eternity, I was eager to see if one of the readings would confirm it, but upon seeing that the Psalm appointed for the day was #72, I didn't think there would be anything. I had spent a summer searching the *Methodist Hymnal* for hymns based on Psalms and then analyzing them. One of these was

"Jesus Shall Reign Where'er the Sun" by the seventeenth century hymnwriter, Isaac Watts. It is from the collection in which Watts "tries to make David speak like a Christian" and is sung to a sweeping melody called *Duke Street*. I had picked that hymn apart, relating each phrase to its scriptural origin, and thought there could not possibly be anything new in Psalm 72 for me. We ought never to assume we "know" any passage of scripture, because there is more in every verse than we can ever comprehend. I read through the psalm somewhat absentmindedly, but when I came to verses twelve through fourteen, I did a double-take. What was that I just read?

> He will deliver the needy when he cries,
> The poor also and him who has no helper.
> He will spare the poor and needy,
> And will save the souls of the needy.
> He will redeem their life from oppression and violence.
> And precious shall be their blood in his sight.

It was talking about Bubba! My sister had said that Bubba was such a needy person, and this scripture said the Lord would spare the needy and save their souls. I could hardly believe it. Each line built upon the previous one in confirmation that this was a message about Bubba. Again, I was awed. The Lord had used his written word to answer a question I had asked Him.

I once heard former astronaut, moonwalker, and current Christian, Charlie Duke, say, in telling about a death in his family, "The Lord does not want his children in the dark; he wants us to *know* about these things." That was surely true for me. He didn't want me going around worrying about Bubba, and he found a way to let me know that he was all right.

As soon as I realized I had heard from the Lord, a spiritual I have taught many times to fourth graders popped into my mind: *Peter, go ring the bells, I heard from heaven today.* Remarkably, those words are the refrain to a verse that says: *I wonder where my brother has gone?* I don't know what its original meaning was, but it has its own meaning for me now. I went around singing it for days.

15

A Glimpse of the Upper Side

On a bright, clear April afternoon, Horace and I checked in at the Aggieland Hotel on the edge of Texas A&M University for our first Parents' Weekend. Within minutes after we called Glenn at his dorm, he arrived to hurry us along to what he called "an event". When I asked what kind of event, he answered, "An aerial view of the campus." Dear Lord, I thought in consternation, he's going to take us up in an airplane.

Glenn had been interested in airplanes all his life, and when he was in high school took flying lessons at Lakeside Airport near where we live. The previous fall, I had rejoiced with him when he passed the tests for his Private Pilot's license. I could accept his flying, but my enthusiasm didn't extend to going up with him. All the way out to Easterwood Airport, sitting in the back seat of his little maroon Scirocco, I secretly prayed that the planned excursion would somehow be prevented. I thought my prayers had been answered when the battery in the plane reserved for us was dead, but, to my chagrin, they took one from another plane. Soon we were speeding down the runway in a Cessna 172 and I was envisioning the next day's headlines: *Family of Three Wiped Out in Plane Crash.* I relaxed as it became apparent that Glenn knew exactly what he was doing, and we had a delightful time touring the area for nearly an hour, the only moment of tension coming when the door next to Horace's seat started to come open.

The next year, when Glenn was a sophomore, he was notified that a pilot slot was reserved for him in the Air Force. All he needed to do was to finish school with a decent grade point average and stay out of trouble. His heavy right foot nearly did him in on the second requirement. The Air Force is rigidly intolerant of "civil involvements" on the part of its prospective officers, and speeding tickets fall into that category. During a spring vacation when he had used up all the grace they offer in that department, Glenn was driving back to Texas from Mississippi when he called to tell me he had just blown his career in Louisiana. Coming into a little town on Highway 165, he had failed to notice a sign saying "Speed Limit 50 miles per hour" and drove out of town with a ticket.

Making a conscious effort not to despair, as I was inclined to do, I reminded him that if the Lord wanted him to be an Air Force pilot, no speeding ticket was going to stand in his way. I knew, though, that the ticket was a big problem, and that familiar knot of anxiety dutifully appeared in my stomach. Glenn decided to throw himself on the mercy of the court, and on his assigned day to appear, I took a day off from school and we drove to central Louisiana. The judge's rulings in the cases preceding ours showed that he was no pushover. The only mercy he gave was extra time in which to pay fines. I had alerted my praying friends to pray for a favorable outcome, and as Glenn made his plea, I was sending up rocket prayers. He acknowledged his fault in exceeding the speed limit, explained its consequence to his career, and asked that the offense not be recorded. The judge listened attentively, told him he believed his story, assessed only court costs, and dropped the charges. When he announced his ruling, I said under my breath, "Praise the Lord." A young black woman sitting in front of me turned around with a big smile on her face and said, "Yeah!" Then I noticed that the whole courtroom was smiling—even people who had been judged by the book. And it seemed that God was smiling on Glenn's plans. Needless to say, he became a reformed driver.

His career seemed in jeopardy again just before graduation when he called me in panic to say he had misunderstood the due-date on a major project and saw no way to complete it on time. The professor was not one to extend mercy. I again alerted my prayer partners, he worked through the night, and graduation came off as scheduled.

At a private commissioning ceremony in the office of the Commandant of the Corps of Cadets, Col. Art Leatherwood, his father's colleague in the 4028th Strategic Reconnaissance Squadron, administered the oath of office and I pinned a pair of gold Second Lieutenant's bars on his shoulders. Sharing the occasion were his grandfather, Joe Hyde, and aunt, Betty Anne Ware, who came from Georgia; my mother from Mississippi; Maxine Leatherwood, who accompanied Art from Austin; and Horace and I. It was a momentous day, evoking a wide range of emotions for us all, but the one I was most conscious of was gratitude. I knew it represented an answer to many prayers.

In the euphoria of reaching this important milestone, I didn't let my thoughts dwell on the nature of Glenn's chosen work. It had struck me with full force the previous winter when he came to Bear Creek School, where I work, to talk to our fifth graders about a career in the armed services. To my unbiased eyes, he was stunningly impressive standing in his Corps of Cadets uniform and shining senior boots addressing a room full of wide-eyed, attentive children who, in most circumstances, acted as if they knew everything there is to know about everything. Part of his presentation was a film of some Air Force jets doing acrobatic flying. That old feeling of exhilaration mixed with pride that I used to get from watching airplanes when my husband was a pilot was welling up in me when I heard Glenn say, "That's what I'll be doing next year." *Oops!* I hadn't really thought about that. Having a husband fly around in those awesome machines had been one thing; but my child, my shining light—this was different! I wasn't sure I was ready for that.

I faced the problem head-on a short time later when Glenn called me at school to tell me he was about to fly a Cessna from College Station to Hooks Airport on the north side of Houston. His truck had been stolen from a shopping center parking lot in southwest Houston during the Christmas holidays and had just been found in a field in north Harris County. The extensive repair it needed could not be started until he brought the title to prove the vehicle belonged to him. Hence the flying trip. I reacted in my usual neurotic way. Why had he told me about it beforehand? There must be some danger associated with the trip that I wasn't aware of—and on and on. My mind told me my fear was irrational, but my soul was in turmoil. I knew that if I reacted like this to such a simple trip, I would go crazy when he started flying jets, and I knew what I was going to have to do. Locking myself in the rest room behind the teacher's lounge, I held out my hands palms up and released Glenn to the care of God in the Prayer of Relinquishment I had learned about from Catherine Marshall a quarter of a century ago. Time had not altered the authenticity of or need for that spiritual act. It freed me to be able to participate with him in reaching his goals.

Pilot training proved to be an even bigger challenge than graduating with a commission. I knew every time he had an important check ride and devoted one whole summer to praying him through them. At one point, it looked as if the answer was going to be that a career in the Air Force was not for him, even though this had been his only goal since he first started planning for his future. When I suggested that there might be a Plan B, he informed me in no uncertain terms that there was no Plan B. The most crucial test came when he was scheduled for a ride that would determine whether or not he would remain in the flight training program. I knew he was in God's hands and that if he failed, there would be something else for him, so I was willing to leave the outcome with Him. At the same time, I knew how desperate Glenn was to succeed and could hardly bear to see him face a crushing disappointment. On the day of the all-important flight, my heart was in my throat. I enlisted all the prayer helpers I could find. Chief among them were Margaret and Kay Graves, who took an interest in Glenn as if he were their own. I had met Margaret in Bible Study Fellowship and we became good friends right away, drawn together by our

A Glimpse of the Upper Side 187

Mississippi backgrounds, our Aggie connection (Hers is a three-generation A&M family), and our love for the Lord. Even after they moved from my neighborhood to Tomball, an hour's drive away, we stayed in close touch. I knew when I called them with a prayer need about Glenn, they understood it. Kay even took the request to his men's prayer group. My journal entry on the day of his test reflects the tension I felt:

> Glenn is to take a ride today that will determine whether or not he remains in the flight training program and the Air Force. I *know* the Lord is in control, but I am having a hard time getting rid of the symptoms of anxiety. I just feel in my heart of hearts that he is supposed to follow this path. My mind has been flooded with verses of assurance but I seem to be afraid to claim them. This I *know*, whether I feel it or not, that He is able to keep that which I have committed unto Him. Psalm 145:18-19 says, "The Lord is near to all who call upon Him, to all who call upon him in truth. He will fulfill the desire of those who fear him." Well, my desire is certainly that Glenn pass this ride today.

In the middle of the day, I went to Noonday Prayers at St. Paul's Church. When they were over, I stopped our Lay Pastoral Assistant, Dick Cavnar, and asked him to pray with me. We went into his office and he took my cold, clammy hands in his and prayed a wonderful, specific prayer for Glenn's success —for his hands, his brain, and his nervous system. I placed the outcome in God's hands, but remained so nervous I was good for nothing when I got home. At the time Glenn was due to take off, I took his Golden Retriever, McArthur, and went for a walk in the scorching July sun. Late that afternoon, the phone rang, and when I answered, a buoyant voice on the other end announced, "I made it!" There have been few times when I have been as relieved or grateful as I was then. The next morning when Glenn walked into his squadron, he got a standing ovation. If anyone wondered how he made such a turnaround, I could have told them. It was just another evidence of the direct hand of God.

Another crucial stage came when he was due for his final check ride in the T-38. He had gotten through the program fine, but had used up all his "second chance" rides. He had to pass this one on the first time out. There was no indication that he might not do this, but something can always go wrong, my anxious mind reasoned. I marshaled the forces that had been so faithful in holding this enterprise up in prayer and went about my business on the day of this last test. (Those forces even included the fifth grade class my sister, Rachel, taught at Woodland Hills School in Jackson—not a public school, it goes without saying.) After school that Friday afternoon, I met Horace at a cafeteria in Houston for supper and we went to the Church of the Holy Spirit for a monthly gathering of the west Houston Cursillo community. When we got home that night, the light on the answering machine was blinking. Not without trepidation, I pushed the button and heard, "Can you believe it? Can you believe that Joe Hyde, the guy who almost washed out of UPT (Undergraduate Pilot Training) took a check ride with the toughest examiner on the base and got an *excellent*? Can you believe it?" Yes, I could believe it. We had prayed simply that he pass, but our God, who is able to do exceeding abundantly above all that we ask or think, had done just that.

A month later, Horace and I drove to Oklahoma for graduation at Vance AFB. The celebration was made even more special for us sunbelt dwellers when a late winter storm left everything covered with snow on our first night there. Sitting in the base theater, where the ceremony took place, we heard the speaker refer to the young people about to receive their wings as the "cream of American youth." He wouldn't get any argument on that from the crowd gathered there. I was surprised to see how many of the new pilots had fathers who had been pilots before them. This was noted as each received his or her wings. When Glenn's name was called, the announcer said, "Lt. Hyde is receiving the wings worn by his father, Capt. Joe G. Hyde, Jr." It's a good thing I was kneeling in the aisle with my face hidden behind a camera, because I was overcome with emotion at that point. Later, I pinned on his wings. I don't know that they were the same ones his father had taken off and given to me on our first date thirty-one years before, but they were definitely of the same vintage—heavy, silver ones unlike those made today.

In one of my Bibles is a treasured book mark given to me in 1965 by Ruth Hyde, my mother-in-law. Woven into it is a picture of a weaver's loom and the following verse:

> *Not till the loom is silent*
> *And the shuttles cease to fly,*
> *Shall God unroll the canvas*
> *And explain the reason why:*
> *The dark threads are as needful*
> *In the Weaver's skillful hand,*
> *As the threads of gold and silver*
> *In the pattern He has planned.*

It seemed to me as I sat in that auditorium on that cold March day in 1988 that I was being permitted to catch a glimpse of the upper side of the canvas spoken of in that poem, even as the weaving continued. I became aware in a new way of the significance of my life as I recalled events in 1957 surrounding my marriage to the father of the young man who had just walked across the stage. How could we have known then that three decades later another Air Force pilot, his son, would be wearing his wings and that he wouldn't be there. We were just two kids in love and not at all mindful of the consequences in history of our committing to each other. Those events were significant far beyond anything we thought of then. My mind began to formulate ideas I wanted to share with my first husband—thoughts about purpose in life. His reason for living seemed to have been to father a child and to leave him a heritage; mine, at least partially, was to bear and nurture that child and pass the heritage on to him. Then Glenn's untimely death didn't seem like the tragedy I always considered it to be. At this point, it was really all right. He died doing the thing he loved doing and that most represented who he was. Dying in the service of his country while performing a sensitive operation caused him to receive public recognition and honor, and this helped to crystallize his heritage. Then there was all the good will he left. Everyone who knew him loved him. (He may have had some enemies, but I didn't know anything about them.) His death, coinciding as it did with what appeared to be culmination of his life, could be looked upon as a gift. In a way I can't explain or understand, I think it was.

The unexpected thing I found out that morning was that I still loved my first husband. When finally I had let him go six years after his death in order to get on with my own life, I thought I had let go of my love for him as well. Now, all these years later, I found that love still tucked away in my heart, and it was like stumbling upon a treasure. My love for him was still intact, and the remarkable thing was that it didn't compete with my love for the big-hearted, good man sitting next to me. Glenn told me on more than one occasion that if anything should happen to him, I should re-marry. I didn't think I would be able to love anyone else, but he always insisted that I could. I wished I could let him know he was right. At the same time, I felt somehow that he did know and that he was pleased.

His last words to me had been "Take care of yourself and the bambino." At this juncture, I realized that I had completed the assignment of caring for the "bambino". For better or worse, he was on his own now. As for myself, the God who had been in my yesterdays would likewise be in the unknown tomorrows.

A new era dawned for me the next morning when Horace, my lover and companion for the long haul, and I turned our Volvo south toward home. Lt. Hyde wasn't the only one who had graduated. I too had completed a job and was satisfied with the outcome. A whole new pattern was about to be woven into the tapestry that is my life, and I knew I could trust the Master Weaver with the rest of it.

Epilogue

Here I raise mine Ebenezer,
Hither by thine help I'm come,
And I hope by thy good pleasure
Safely to arrive at home.[1]

It is now 1996, ten years since the idea for this book was conceived, six since the final period was entered. I just read it afresh, with some detachment, and the thing that strikes me is that it is like a collection of *ebenezers*. No, the word doesn't mean *miser*, or anything connected with Mr. Scrooge. It is a Hebrew word meaning *stone of help*. The prophet Samuel erected an ebenezer to commemorate an Israeli routing of the Philistines and said, "Thus far the LORD has helped us." It seems to me that every time we recognize the help of God in our lives and mark it in some way, we are raising an ebenezer. And of course, one way to mark it is to write it down. That's the first benefit I see from making the effort to record significant spiritual events. It strengthens our faith and reminds

---

[1] from the hymn *Come Thou Fount of Every Blessing* by Robert Robinson (1735-1790), unaltered version.

us that He who has begun a good work in us will bring it to completion.

I think it was Socrates who said the unreflected life is not worth living. I certainly wouldn't argue with Socrates, but I don't *know* that he is absolutely correct in this. What I do know is that the reflected life is indeed of great value, especially if the reflection takes into account the work of God in one's life. I have habitually engaged in some examination and interpretation of my life, but the process of looking at it as a whole and setting it down in some kind of order gave me freedom and insight that I consider major benefits of the reflected life.

First, there was the freedom of not having to keep remembering all the things I wanted to leave with my family so they would know where they came from. I found out how much I have already forgotten when I re-read this manuscript and kept running across things I didn't know I knew. By putting it down in writing, I've deleted a lot of information to make room for more memory in my brain— a good thing, since I don't think it will get an upgrade any time soon.

The insight came from seeing God's hand so consistently at work in the direction my life has taken. Somehow, tying it all together made it undeniably believable. Whole new worlds have opened up since I tied a ribbon round my first half century and put it on the shelf.

Within a year, Judy Parma joined our family as the perfect helpmate for my son, Glenn. She had been my choice for a long time before he realized she was the right one. His first assignment after pilot training was as a B-52 co-pilot stationed on Guam. When he spent a few days at home before taking off for the Pacific, I saw no evidence of contact with Judy, but I did have the grace to hold my peace. Several months later, I was in Austin, where Judy lived, and gave her a call. What a surprise it was to hear her answering machine say, "I can't talk right now; I'm in Guam." Still I held my peace, but it wasn't easy, as Glenn and I were communicating almost daily with little messages of E-mail. Then came the day I turned on the computer and read, "I think I'm going to get married." *(Hallelujah! The boy finally waked up and smelled the coffee.)* And thus began a new and delightful chapter in my life.

They were married in a beautiful Catholic ceremony in Judy's home church in Arlington. Glenn had definite ideas about the music he wanted for the wedding, and Judy and her family graciously turned over that part of the planning to him. It became a family project. He had heard a high school band play the variations on "Simple Gifts" from Aaron Copland's *Appalachian Spring* in a marching contest in Austin and had his heart set on having it played by a brass quartet. The nearest to such an arrangement we could find was one for nine strings. So Horace, bless him, sat down at the computer and transcribed it for brass and keyboard. Our cousin, Margaret Ingram, a professional musician in north Texas, hired the brass players and put it all together along with some lovely arrangements of her own, including a lot of Bach. Ten bridesmaids entered to the peaceful strains of *Sheep May Safely Graze.* The matron-of-honor, and then the bride, were heralded by the Copland work. Judy walking down the long aisle on the arm of her father as the final variation played in all its grandeur was breathtaking. Later in the service, Horace sang *Ave Maria* and it was so beautiful it brought tears to many Catholic eyes plus mine. There was a lot to bring tears to my eyes, but they were happy tears.

For our stay in Arlington, we set up headquarters in a hotel across the road from Six Flags Over Texas and welcomed kinfolk from far and wide. Glenn's cousin, Nate, interrupted his schedule as a resident at Vanderbilt to come and be in the wedding. A slew of cousins on the Hyde side came, including Jeff, one of the twins whose physiques were so admired by their father and uncle when they were babies. Both grandparents, my mother and Mr. Hyde, came, as well as aunts and uncles on both sides and another cousin, my niece, Katie. We celebrated with the bride and groom and saw them off to their new home in Marquette, Michigan—a little too far away to suit me, but it did give them an opportunity to start their life together in peace.

At about the same time, Horace suddenly found himself in what seemed to be the perfect job—one he really liked with a small young company that was thriving. After a somewhat uncertain time due to the shaky Houston economy during the eighties, this was an unexpected state of security, and I began to see that it would be possible for me to retire from teaching. I enjoyed the children and hadn't given any thought to leaving my job, but the work load and pressure increased every year and I seemed to gather new interests on the outside at the same rate, so I decided to take the plunge and end my career slightly ahead of schedule.

Those outside interests included heavy involvement in the music ministry of my church. By this time, Horace had found his musical home in the choir at Holy Spirit Episcopal Church in Houston and even served as interim director during their search for a new choirmaster. I, too, loved that church, especially since my friend from the summer of '73 at Laity Lodge, Melvin

Gray, was rector. But I felt drawn to the little community at St. Paul's Church in Katy, and especially to the rector's vision of the role of music in worship.

My musical background is classical and no one loves the great musical tradition of historic Christianity more than I. One of the peculiar ways I spend my time is in studying hymns. I love researching the theology behind the words and then singing—and playing—them to good strong tunes. And I don't hesitate to take issue with modern hymn editors who, in the name of relevance, replace words like *ebenezer*, so rich in imagery and biblical connotation, with innocuous everyday words that can mean anything. All this is to say that my attachment to church music is visceral. Not surprisingly, I took a dim view of guitar music in church. Then I encountered renewal music in the Episcopal Church. (Horace's viscera still react negatively to such; that's why he went to the big church in the city: he *thought* he was getting away from it!)

My prejudice began to change shortly after we joined St. Paul's Episcopal Church when a lady there gave me a tape of music by a group that grew out of that denomination called *The Fisherfolk*. I was polite and promised to listen to it during a drive to Mississippi, while secretly planning to get it over with as soon as possible and move on to my own tapes. What actually happened was that I couldn't turn off the *Fisherfolk* tape. It played almost non-stop for nine hours while I sang along, praising God and pondering the scripture that served as text. I saw in that music a powerful vehicle for getting people involved in worship. It was simple enough to be accessible to nearly everyone but not lacking in vitality and artistry. The words were strong and dignified, not sentimental as I had expected. It was altogether satisfying to me. I began to envision worship services in which traditional hymns and anthems were supplemented with, not replaced by, renewal music. The upshot of this was that I ended up leading the music program at St. Paul's, beginning with directing the choir and playing the organ. Later a children's choir was added, plus a couple of days teaching music in the day school. Time on my hands after retirement was not a problem.

Then came the summer of 1990, and Saddam Hussein decided to try to take over Kuwait. Suddenly, names of places many of us had never heard of began to dominate the news and engender fear and foreboding in the citizenry. Having a son in the armed services made me especially sensitive to the threat of war, but I really didn't think there was a chance of his being involved. He was barely established in his new job in Michigan, and the bomber model they flew there was not likely to be used in a conflict like the one brewing in the Middle East.

By late January of the following year, Desert Shield had become Desert Storm and the process of bombing the daylights out of Iraq was underway. I was at a women's retreat at Laity Lodge, enjoying warm fellowship with new and old friends and experiencing the novelty of winter, complete with glistening, crackling trees, in a place I had known only in summer. There couldn't have been a better place to be when I got a call from Glenn on about the third night. He called to say that two crews from his base were being deployed to a staging area for bombing missions in the war, and his was one of them. How quickly one's world can turn upside down! And how cared for I was to be in the midst of people who were tuned in to the Source of our very life and passed that assurance on to me through their prayers and concern. (One of my secret fears is of having to face a major crisis by myself with no one around for support. That has never, ever happened to me in any such event. I think it's time I turned that one loose—if only I could persuade my viscera to do the same.)

The next weeks are a blur to me. I do remember one Sunday morning when someone in the choir happened to mention as we were doing a quick warm-up that a B-52 had gone down as it returned from a mission over Iraq. I was about to start the prelude when Ellis Brust, our rector, walked by on his way to vest. I stopped him and told him what I had just heard, then said "I know Glenn is just as safe in his plane as he is at home, because he's in God's hands both places, but I can't help worrying." He laid his hands on my shoulders and prayed right there in front of God and everybody for Glenn's safety and my peace, and then he said he had seen an angel holding up an airplane as he prayed. (It must have been a big angel if it was holding up a B-52.) I didn't think too much about the angel at the time, but I did tell Glenn about it, and it made a big impression on his crew, as his aircraft commander's mother had had a similar vision.

I also remember the night in March when President Bush announced the war's end. I didn't hear the speech because I was at the piano for our Wednesday night prayer and praise service when it was aired, but I found out later that Glenn listened to it from the co-pilot's seat in the cockpit of his plane on the return trip from Iraq to his base on an island in the Indian Ocean. His crew had arrived on the scene just in time to fly the last B-52 mission of the war. Mercifully, that news didn't reach me ahead of time and I had blithely assumed that the war ended before he got there. Compared to what millions of mothers through the centuries have had to endure during wartime, this wasn't much of a trial, for which I am grateful. It was surely enough of one for me.

The year 1991 ended just as it began—in crisis. In December rain came to southeast Texas and stayed. Relentlessly it poured, dripped, and soaked right through the holidays, and we sprang a leak in our roof next to the chimney. That's why there were buckets strategically placed in our attic on the day after Christmas when I was busy wallpapering our bedroom. Some little errand took me into the living room just in time to hear a monstrous, crashing noise coming from above the ceiling. When I went to look, I found a water-filled bucket lodged precariously in the chimney well. This struck me as an emergency, so I called Horace at work and he came home to see about it. He left his briefcase open in his office and his computer turned on, never dreaming when he pulled out of the parking lot that it would be two months before he would be back.

How quickly one's world can turn upside down. That's what happened to us after the bucket had been retrieved and repositioned and we had eaten a bite of lunch. Sitting at the kitchen table, Horace had a heart attack—just like that. One minute everything was normal, and the next he was fighting for his life. An ambulance came and took him to the hospital. I met them there after making one phone call, and people began arriving from two churches. One of the first to come was my friend, Sharon Turner, associate rector at Holy Spirit, gifted pastor, and bearer of light and plain good sense. She stuck by me like glue for the next three weeks. Horace's doctor, Mark Bing, kept coming out to the waiting room with bleak reports, full of words like vascular disease, diabetes, arrhythmia, shocks, and something about a tunnel. Finally I said, "Well, Mark, we're just going to pray," to which he replied, "I think that's a real good idea." And we did. And they got him stabilized.

Darkness had fallen by the time they moved him to intensive care, and we all moved upstairs to the dreary little waiting room across the hall. A little incident occurred there during those tense hours of waiting, not knowing which way things would go, that I have turned over in my mind many times since. The Lord must have meant it when he said "A merry heart doeth good like a medicine"[2] because He provided some merry medicine for us. Sharon had gone back into Houston and when she rejoined us in the ICU waiting room, she brought some sandwiches. In the meantime, someone else had brought sandwiches, and for some reason Sharon started apologizing for using buns instead of sliced bread for hers. Forbes Baker set off a volcano of laughter when he said, "Sharon, your buns are just fine." The next thing we saw was someone from down the hall closing our door. We must have seemed pretty raucous to be keeping a hospital vigil. But I think it showed the winsomeness and tenderness of the Lord to provide that respite from the heaviness. I have thought about this more recently since reading a book by Frederick Buechner in which he mentions Jesus Christ being crowned over and over in the hearts of His people "among confession, and tears, and great laughter."[3] Somehow, I think that applies to the scene I'm trying to describe here—a moment of grace in the midst of our earthiness. The gloom lifted like fog burning off in the morning sun, and when I was finally allowed to go in and see Horace, I was refreshed and

---

[2] Proverbs 17:22.
[3] Frederick Buechner, *Listening to Your Life* (San Francisco: HarperCollins, 1992) p. 23.

able to encourage him. He looked so pitiful hooked up to all those wires and bleeping machines. But we had a good laugh about the buns and he enjoyed hearing that he was providing the occasion for such a good party for his friends.

And then the Lord pronounced a benediction on the evening by sending another priest, the third one of the day. The first two were my pastor, Ellis, and Sharon from Horace's church. I was on the phone in ICU talking to Glenn, who tracked me down there after I left him a message, and looked up to see Hubert Palmer, rector emeritus of Holy Spirit and father of my friend, Timmie Eubanks, walk in. The grapevine had apparently reached Timmie's house and Hubert was visiting, so they came. It meant a lot to both of us when he prayed for Horace. I heard later that when someone opened the door to the waiting room and Hubert saw who was there, he said "I can see this is a rough crowd."

Well, rough or gentle, depending on one's point of view, the crowd dispersed around nine o'clock, and I went to spend my first night home alone in many a moon. I made sure the ringer on the phone was turned on, curled up in bed like a baby, and just asked Jesus to hold me. I had never seriously considered the idea of losing Horace. He was so strong and healthy and absolutely dependable that I had just taken him for granted. It took this calamity for me to see how much he meant to me, and I was like a helpless child. Jesus must have held me, because sleep came easily and I woke up the next morning grateful that the phone had refrained from ringing during the night.

Three weeks later, Horace came home from the hospital with five free-flowing arteries grafted with veins from other parts of his body, and he began a

Epilogue 203

flawless process of recovery. I dropped all my outside commitments and devoted my energies to learning to cook healthful food and maintaining a calm (and as orderly as I can manage) household. It had been over thirty years since I had been "just a housewife", and I found the job suited me just fine—especially when I stepped into the added role of grandmother. Shelby Anne Hyde arrived in 1993.

I saw her in October when she was about two weeks old. Judy uncovered her little bundle in the airport in Marquette, and there was a beautiful little face with eyes just like her father's and grandfather's. A grandmother has so many things to ponder in her heart.

There was more to ponder the next morning. In a little ceremony after mass, Shelby Anne wore the christening gown that had been worn by her mother and grandmother and was established in the household of God. As a little circle of friends, including her two grandmothers, looked on, Father Brown baptized her in the name of the Father, the Son, and the Holy Spirit. She screamed to high heaven about an earthly thing, her overdue lunch, as she was sealed by the Holy Spirit in Baptism and marked as Christ's own forever—a heavenly thing. And I thought of the time to come when she would receive Jesus through her own faith, because that time will come; it will be the focus of my prayers for her, as it has been since before she was born.

A few weeks later we were all in Mississippi for the holidays with my mother. On the night Horace and I drove in, we went to Shoney's for supper. While we were there, it occurred to me that around the table in that inauspicious setting sat the five people most dear to me in all the world. There was Mama, bright, spunky, charming lady who had become like a best friend to me. And Horace, faithful companion, sometimes teddy bear, sometimes grizzly, both lovable. Then Glenn, handsome boy, still the light of my life. Then there was Judy, beautiful wife and mother and good friend to her mother-in-law. And now Shelby—well, we've all heard enough about grandchildren, so suffice it to say she is a precious child. There they were—my inner circle, the most significant of all the "others" in my life. It was a defining moment to see them as special gifts from God that had been entrusted to me, and to realize that in a non-burdensome way, I am responsible for them.

Exercising that responsibility became a good deal more convenient when Glenn was transferred from the shores of Lake Superior to the banks of the Rio Grande. Of all the places he could have been sent, it was to Laughlin Air Force Base. Del Rio, the place that has shone like a jewel in my memory since I spent five of the happiest years of my life there, has now become the setting for a new set of memories-in-the-making. Visiting the children there is pure pleasure, like going home—to familiar streets on which a few old friends still reside, and to a granddaughter running in circles around the house when I walk in the door! Could this be coincidence? I'm inclined to think not.

I spent a weekend with Judy and Shelby last year when Glenn was on a cross-country. On Sunday when it was time for him to come home, we went out to the base and parked on the side of the road outside the main gate to watch him do touch-and-go landings in his T-38. Then we went in the gate and down to the flightline to pick him up, stopping at the very spot where I used to drop my first husband off to leave on cross-countries more than three decades ago. It was the spot where, in my dream a few days after his death, I

Epilogue 205

drove to deposit him and where he answered all my spiritual instructions with the flat announcement that he had already seen Jesus. It seemed almost surreal that I was there, all these years later, sitting in that same spot, under that same wide, southwest Texas sky, looking out on the same landing field with our grandchild next to me and waiting for our son to come in from the same. All I could think was "Look what the Lord has done for me!" An ebenezer.

Skirting around the east side of Del Rio is a street called Bedell, familiar to me because I used to travel it every day to my job at East Side School. During that time in the early sixties I watched the Val Verde Memorial Hospital take shape across the street from where I worked. One Sunday afternoon when it was brand new I went there to receive a brand new medicine—a vaccine for poliomyelitis, the dreaded disease the threat of which hung like the sword of Damocles over my generation when we were growing up. I went with all the young people of the city to get the protection administered on a cube of sugar. I expected never to have a reason to set foot in that hospital again, but the occasion did arise many years later in 1996. Stopping there on my way into town on a June evening that year, I walked to the maternity ward to see Judy and little Hayden Glenn, who had been born that morning. An eight-pound baby is not a small one, but he seemed so little all bundled up like a papoose with a knit cap on his head. Before my visit in Del Rio was over, I could see that he has a beautiful little face and eyes that puff up when he cries, like his dad's did, so he must have those Hyde eyes. And he surely has a proud and grateful grandmother who is so happy to have him in her inner circle of significant others. There was another ebenezer.

In the midst of sailing these smooth, pleasant seas, I learned again for the umpteenth time how little it takes to upset my equilibrium. I have been reluctant to believe that God sends adversity into our lives to shape us up. After all, Jesus did warn that in the world we would have tribulation, and I detect in that the attribution of bad things to the fact that we live in a fallen, broken, godless world that can not be expected to produce anything out of its natural state but evil. On the other hand, Jesus told us to be not dismayed, because he had overcome the world. At this stage in redemptive history, he does not necessarily intervene to prevent trouble from touching us, but we can be sure he is with His own sheep in whatever they face and that he will, in his sovereignty, work everything together for our ultimate good. That's my answer to those who say that bad things happen to good people because God is either too mean or too weak to do anything about it. (That explanation, by the way, is diametrically opposed to what I perceive as two of the most salient attributes of God, his *goodness* and his *omnipotence*.)

The Bible does have a lot to say, however, about the discipline and pruning necessary for growth and fruitfulness to occur in God's children. Some things we consider bad do come to us through the hand of God to teach us. The latest instance of my world turning upside down was, I believe, a case in point.

One August day, without the slightest hint of a warning, Horace became a victim of the modern phenomenon known as corporate downsizing. I immediately took on the mindset of a victim, complaining of the unfairness and hardship and worrying about how we would manage at this stage of life when it was too soon for Horace to retire and too late to find another job easily. I grieved with him over

Epilogue 207

this sundering from his familiar life and relationships at work and passed through each day under a cloud of despair that got darker and heavier as time passed with no developments on the employment front. I felt as if I were confined to a straight jacket with my routine at home messed up, my peace of mind about the future gone, and my spending habits cut back to absolute necessities.

    I've known for a long time that I had never really dealt with my fear of financial insecurity. Threats in that department can evoke near-panic in my spirit. I should have known that the Lord was going to get me past that sooner or later, and that it would probably hurt, but I didn't look at this present situation with spiritual eyes. I just wanted things back the way they used to be—with a happy, fulfilled husband going to work everyday, the house to myself during the day, and an occasional spree at the mall. (I'm not entirely out of sympathy with the parody "when the going gets tough the tough go shopping.") Well, as I chafed and pouted, He found a way to get through to me and teach me a thing or two.

    The Old Testament prophets write about a time when the earth will be full of the knowledge of the Lord as the waters cover the sea. That hasn't happened yet, but just above the surface of the earth, the knowledge of the Lord does hover—in the air waves. Just the flick of a dial can bring the living, active word of God right to one's ears by means of radio. One program I make a point to hear when I can is called *Leading the Way*, featuring the teaching of Michael Youssef. I happened to tune in one morning as he was speaking on the first verses in the book of James—those verses through which the Bible first spoke directly to me so many years ago when I knew next to nothing about such things: *Count it all joy when you fall into various trials.*

I was folding laundry and agreeing with every word as he went through the next verse and expounded on it: *knowing that the testing of your faith produces patience.* I know the Word and can appreciate good teaching, of which this was the best. *(Amen, Brother, preach on!)* Then he moved on to verse 4: *But let patience have its perfect work, that you may be perfect and complete, lacking nothing.* "Do you know what he's saying?" Michael asked, "He's saying don't rebel against your circumstances." *Bullseye!* The Lord himself, through the voice of His preacher, burned with His light of truth straight to the darkest corner of my soul. The living, powerful two-edged sword that is the Word of God had indeed discerned the thoughts and intents of my heart.[4] Rebelling is exactly what I was doing, and I had not even known it. "Allow the testing process to go to completion," Michael continued, "so that you may receive the maximum benefit of God's teaching. If you're constantly rebelling against your circumstances, and all you want and all you can think about is that you get out of your circumstances, you'll never become a mature Christian. You'll never grow." (How 'bout that? I thought I was already a mature Christian.) He went on to point out that God's wisdom is available to the Christian for the asking, and through it we gain God's perspective and are able to learn through difficult times.

There have been few turning points in my faith as dramatic as that one. My mind was renewed in an instant. The thought that God cared enough for me to send such a direct word changed my attitude from one

---

[4] Hebrews 4:12.

of rebellion to thanksgiving. Suddenly, I knew He had our situation in hand and I was at peace. I knew He would provide for us, though not necessarily in the way I envisioned. Whatever happened in regard to a job, all would be well. "All manner of things would be well."[5]

Nevertheless, this is not the end of the story, as it didn't take long for me to backslide from that pinnacle of faith. I can identify with St. Paul when he writes that when he wants to do good, evil is close at hand.[6] On a fair autumn day, Horace had gone to Houston to interview for a job he went on to take when it was offered to him. I was performing the daily and mundane task of making the bed and ruminating about the most grievous trial I was being required to endure when a set of heretical ideas began to assault my mind: *God is not really concerned with our everyday life. He'll take care of us when we die, but He has other things to occupy His attention than the little petty details we worry about. If anything turns out right, it's just luck, being in the right place at the right time, or because of our own ability. And the things that go wrong? Well, He is not even aware of those. But He will save us when we die.* I began to draw implications from this sad state of affairs, ending with me at an advanced age without so much as two cents to rub together. Then suddenly, I came to myself and recognized the source of those blasphemous thoughts as none other than our ancient foe. And I was mad! How dare that old snake try to trip up a child of the King with that trash!

I had to role play a confrontation with the devil years ago when I was Miss Appleby in my senior class play, *The Devil and Miss Appleby*, at Leland High School. The part of my nemesis was played, not

---

[5] Julian of Norwich, *Revelations of Divine Love*.
[6] Romans 7:21.

inappropriately, I might mention, by a boy named Arlen. He made my part harder with all kinds of devilment of his own on stage, like poking me in the rear with his pitchfork when the director wasn't looking. Frances Smith, senior English teacher and play director, ruled with an iron hand and wouldn't let us get away with anything less than her high standards. One night I showed up at rehearsal in blue jeans and a Camp Montreat sweatshirt, and we set to work on a line I was supposed to deliver with such aplomb that it sent the devil packing: *Get thee behind me, Satan.* Poor Miss Smith! She tried, but she didn't get out of me what she wanted that night. Finally, she said in exasperation, "Marianne, don't you ever come to practice dressed like that again. You don't look like Miss Appleby, you don't sound like Miss Appleby, and you don't feel like Miss Appleby."

Well, I probably didn't look like Miss Appleby the morning I confronted Satan in my bedroom, but I surely had her authority, if not her class, when I blurted out to him, "Shut up, you lying devil!"

It makes a funny story to tell now, but something so awesome happened afterward that it melts my heart to this day. Immediately, like a radio coming on in my head, I heard, "Consider the lilies of the field, how they grow. They toil not, neither do they spin, yet Solomon in all his glory was not arrayed like one of these." My mother used to sing a solo to that text and I played the accompaniment. I can remember lying in my berth on the *Panama Limited* rolling along toward Stephens College, unable to sleep, and hearing that song roll through my brain, sort of like sheep jumping over a fence. That's when those words got implanted in my soul. So I went directly to Matthew 6 in a King James Bible and read on:

Epilogue

> *Therefore take no thought, saying, What shall we eat? or What shall we drink? or Wherewithal shall we be clothed? For your heavenly Father knoweth that ye have need of all these things. But seek ye first the kingdom of God, and his righteousness, and all these things shall be added unto you.*[7]

I learned all over again that what the Bible says is true. I had resisted the devil, and he had fled, just as James said he would.[8] And then our gracious Lord had immediately stepped in and fed me exactly the words of His written truth that countered the lies. Satan had set out to turn me away from Jesus and had ended up driving me back into His arms with a deeper faith and greater love.

Even with the profound truths I took in from this experience, the fact remains that I'll never get this life down to where I do it right. None of us ever graduates from the Christian life. We just press on. I'll continue to set my mind on earthly things and get off the track. God in His mercy and love will continue to allow tests that highlight areas of my soul that need to be sanctified. And "Old Scratch" (my grandmother's name for the devil) will be there to try to capitalize. But by the grace of God, I'll keep turning back to the Truth and He will go on perfecting that which concerns me[9]—all that concerns me, including those I love—until we all join the angels and archangels and all the company of heaven around the throne of grace.

Thanks be to God.

---

[7] Matthew 6:31-33.
[8] James 4:7.
[9] Psalm 138:8. (KJV)

A Final Word

A few months after I finished writing the Epilogue, my mother took her place before the throne of grace and added her beautiful voice to the heavenly chorus. During the time when I was coming to terms with my loss, her lifelong friend, Mary Alyce Smith, had a dream about her that was a great comfort to me. She later wrote about it in a devotional booklet compiled in their church, and I asked permission to include it here, because it is so consistent with my experience in dealing with deaths of those close to me. This is what she wrote:

> I lost my friend last year and didn't get to go to her funeral. I was recuperating from heart surgery. She used to come over late in the afternoon at what I call twilight and what B. F. calls "bull-bat' time. Cora said we had the prettiest view of the sunset in town and I agree.
>
> We would talk about life in general and all the wisdom we had acquired and quote bits of poetry—English poets, as well as Bryant's *Thanatopsis*, to Pulitzer Prize winners Edna St. Vincent Millay and Amy Lowell, and above all, the Bible, the greatest book ever written.

> One evening she brought a little book for my coffee table called *Little Bits of Wisdom*. Today it was open to "If you laugh a lot when you get older, your wrinkles will be in the right place." Hers were.
>
> I dreamed one night that I was presiding in Sunday School and looked up to see her sitting in her regular place. I said, "Cora, I thought you had died." She looked at me with that little twinkle in her eye and said, "That's what *you* thought." Marianne, her daughter, said she was letting me know that everything is great and that she is happy. I believe it!

Not even the most faithful saint is impervious to the ancient taunt *Hath God said?*[1] Did he really say that whoever believes in him should not perish but have everlasting life?[2] And if he said it, did he mean what my simple mind interprets it to mean, or was he speaking in some kind of code signifying a lesser comfort? I don't chart my spiritual course by dreams, but I do think they can serve to confirm for us that what we believed all along from knowing the word of God is indeed true. He wants us to *know*. A superior intelligence is not a requirement for interpreting his word. All it takes is a heart that truly wants to know Him, and that, of course, is a gift of grace. It's all grace.

---

[1] Genesis 3:1
[2] John 3:16

Well, this is the third time I've ended this book. Let me get it to the printer fast before I have to end it again. I so appreciate those readers who have come this far with me. I know you have many ways to spend your time, and if you have spent some of it traveling through my life with me, I am honored. If anyone would care to communicate with me, I would love to hear from you. My Internet e-mail address is *mgsmith@wt.net.*

Order Form

Marismith Books
P. O. Box 941446
Houston, Texas 77094-8446

To order *To See His Goodness*, please enclose check or money order for $12.95 plus shipping: $3.00 for one book, $1.00 for each additional book. Texas residents add $.94 sales tax per book.

Name _____

Address _____

City _____ State _____ Zip _____

Or, you may order *To See His Goodness* online at: http://www.toseehisgoodness.com